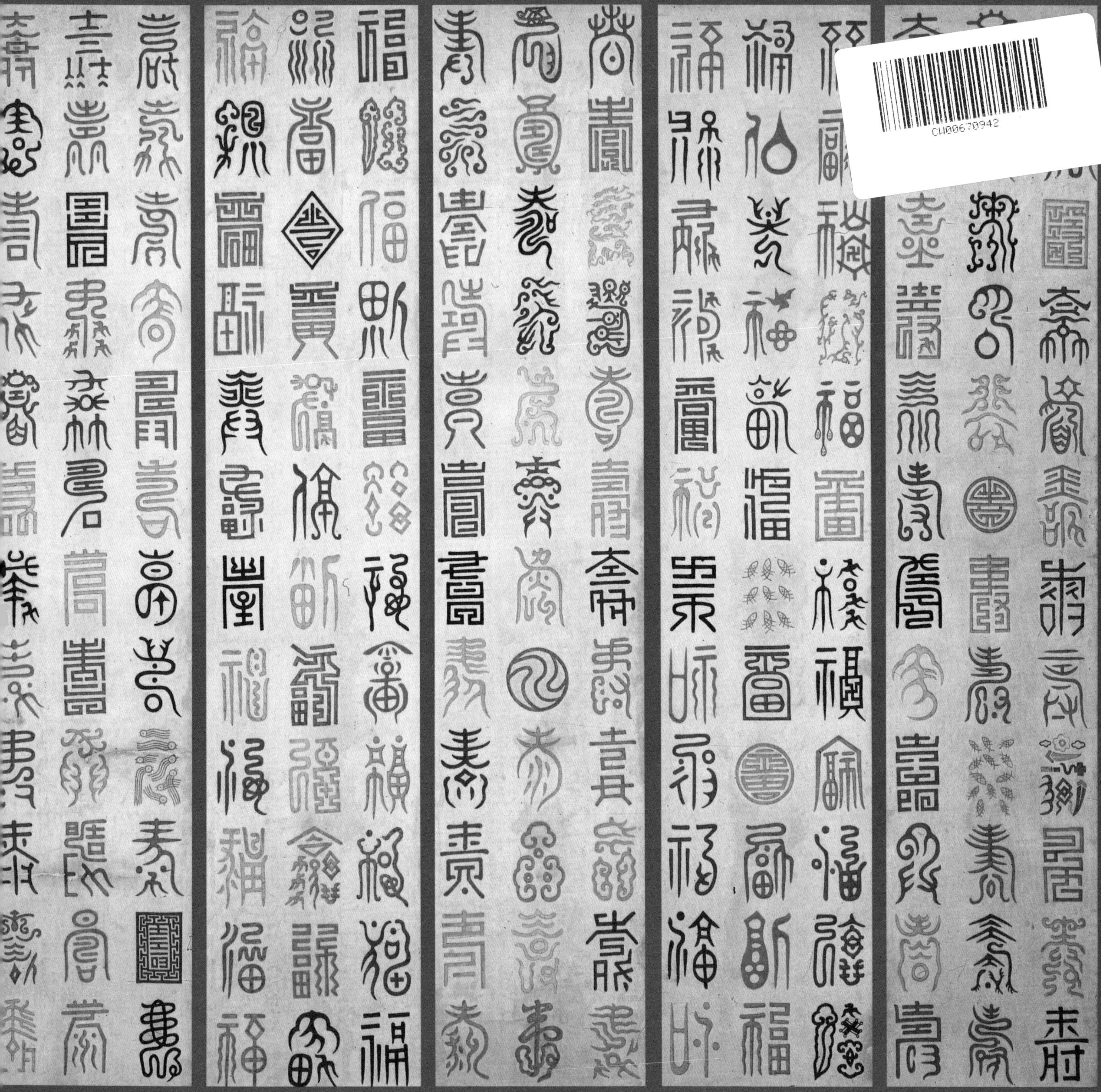

The needle has a spirit,
Apart from its outward traces.
Not fingers nor silk filament,
But by graceful power, a painting is done.

—Ni Renji (China, 1607–1685)

PAINTING WITH A NEEDLE

learning the art of silk embroidery with YOUNG YANG CHUNG

Text and drawings by Young Yang Chung, Ph.D.

Harry N. Abrams, Inc., Publishers

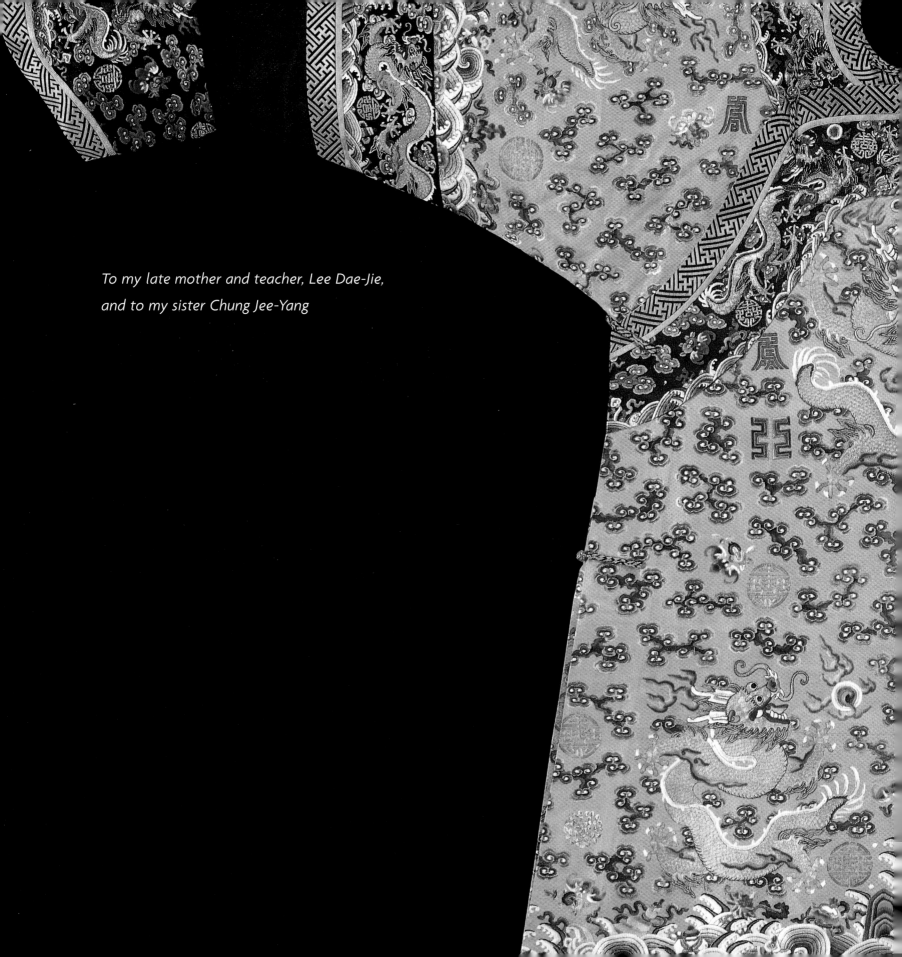

To my late mother and teacher, Lee Dae-Jie,
and to my sister Chung Jee-Yang

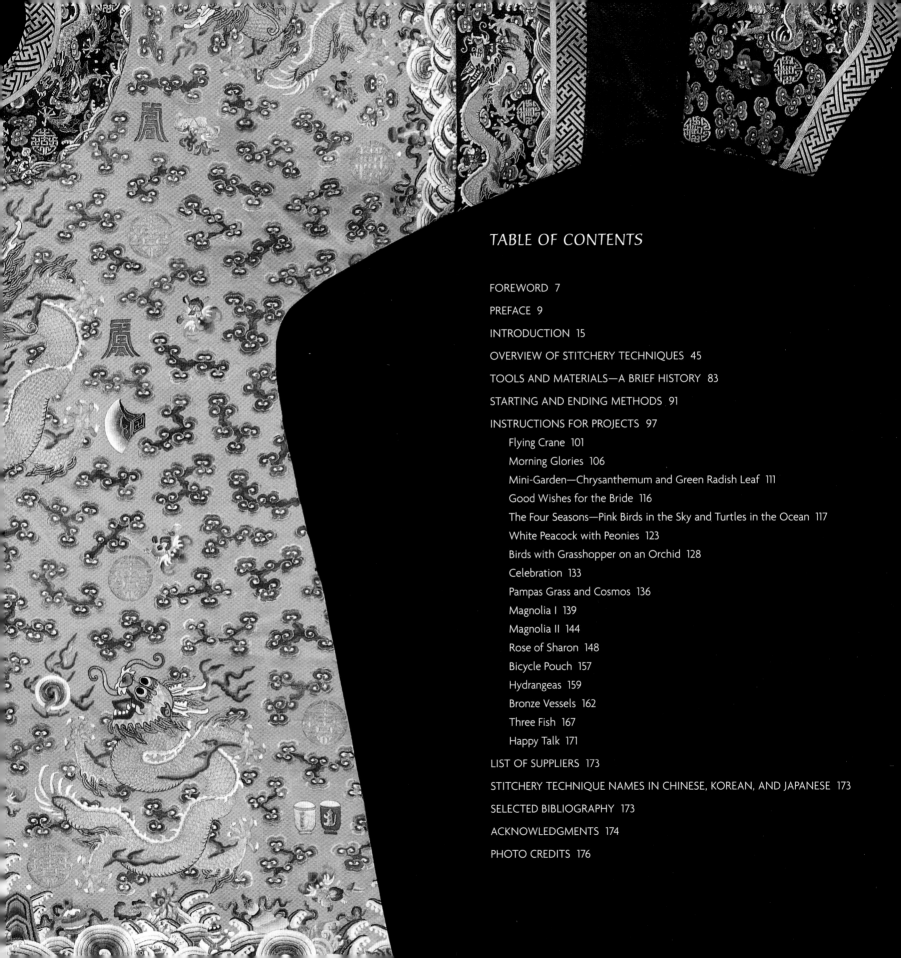

TABLE OF CONTENTS

FOREWORD

For the past thirty years, embroiderers and textile historians focusing on Oriental embroidery have enriched their understanding of East Asian, especially Korean, embroidery through the work of Young Yang Chung.

My first acquaintance with Young Chung occurred early in her career, when I discovered a new publication, *The Art of Oriental Embroidery* (Charles Scribner's Sons, 1979). The focus on history and cultural revelation as well as techniques appealed to me as an embroiderer and as a means of studying the cultures and histories of Korea, Japan, and China. I read and reread the pages, visited exhibits of Asian textiles in the mid-Atlantic region and elsewhere, and pursued opportunities to learn more, inspired and guided by Young Chung's text.

Young Chung has continued her studies and teaching in New York City, Korea, and elsewhere, sharing her expertise through exhibits, articles, and lectures and serving as scholarly adviser to museums and exhibit venues. Her audience includes scholars, embroiderers, needle artists, collectors, and historians. Her most recent book, a catalogue for the May 2000 exhibit on Korean embroidery at Sookmyung Women's University Museum, is a visual feast of embroidery: insignia, bookmarks, folding screens, robes, medicine pouches, eyeglass cases, pillows and cushions, wonderful tasseled pendants, baby hats, hair ornaments, and more. The cranes, tigers, turtles, birds, and flowers provide numerous examples of embroidery integral to cultural events and uses fulfilled through this art.

Little wonder that I felt excitement for all of us as embroiderers when I learned of this newest publication planned by Young Chung. Designed with a focus on techniques for all levels, using accessible, contemporary materials, the book features projects that acknowledge both the Asian and the Western approaches to embroidery, with samples stitched by Asian and American artists. The text offers history, culture, projects, detailed diagrams, and lavish color photography.

Embroiderers and non-embroiderers alike will enjoy this book intellectually and aesthetically, and one look at the how-to projects such as *Rose of Sharon, Morning Glories, Flying Crane,* or *Turtles in the Ocean,* each accompanied by detailed instructions and diagrams, will inspire anyone to take off to the nearest needlework store. By undertaking any one of these projects using 21st-century approaches in techniques and materials, the chasm is bridged between ancient and modern times. And that is Young's intention—to bring the past and present together not only through her own exquisite designs, but by sharing her vast knowledge of the ancient traditions of this spectacular form of art and self-expression.

Marie Campbell
President, The Embroiderers' Guild of America, 2002

Page 1:
White Crane, see caption, page 53

Pages 2–3:
Wedding Robe, detail (Japanese, 19th century). This traditional wedding robe is covered with symbols of longevity (cranes, turtles, bamboo, and plum trees) and happiness (color red). The combination of pine needles and plum blossoms represents marriage. The mythical, dragonlike turtles have heavy padding on their shells, which are covered with couched metallic threads. The wavelike tails are done entirely in outline stitch, and the cranes are completed in satin stitch.

Pages 4–5:
Twelve-Symbol Dragon Robe, see caption, page 36

Opposite:
The author embroidering in her studio. Displayed before her is a variety of threads including, from left: peacock-feather-wrapped thread, untwisted silk thread on spools, and an assortment of metallic threads. She is using the two-hand method—her right hand guides and manipulates the needle beneath the stretcher; her left hand does the same above the stretcher.

PREFACE

The first stitch I ever made was a "button hole" stitch sewn for the five buttons of my father's linen vest, and I consider this initial leap into the world of embroidery to be my first masterpiece. I learned how to sew from my talented mother, who was educated by a home tutor in the traditional Korean manner, and my newfound dexterity brought me great popularity with my fourth-grade schoolmates struggling to cultivate their own embroidery skills. During one summer vacation, I created white doilies as a homework assignment, a project that required three long months of diligent work. My embroidery teacher, Joo Jeong-sook, a beautiful red-haired, blue-eyed Russian, warned me not to rub the embroidered doilies too hard when washing them so that their French-knot stitches would remain fresh and in proper position before I handed them in. I also learned that the outline stitch was good for making stems for the good-luck cloverleaf patterns I embroidered on the corners of handkerchiefs. Once a week my mother hand-washed my father's linen vest by scrubbing it with white soap in cold water, repeating the same phrase, "Be careful with the button holes!" I still vividly recall the French embroidery classes I attended during these childhood years, and I encounter again and again the formidable English names of the stitchery techniques I learned back then whenever I read excavation reports describing archaeological discoveries of early embroideries from various regions in East Asia.

During the Korean War, my family fled Seoul for my father's hometown in Chungchong-do, where I taught young country ladies five to six years my senior to make Western-style, white-on-white embroidered home accessories, such as doilies to place on tables and under flower vases, to include with their marriage dowries. Girls of my age (14 years old) were too young to join this group, but I was thrilled to be accorded respect beyond my years and treated to dried persimmons and homemade rice buns during lessons. From these village women, I learned to make homespun silk threads and to dye them in natural pigment with ashes, and as a group we stitched together every night under the dim light of a single kerosene lamp. As a graduation project from my six-year school program, I spun cotton threads with a homemade spinning wheel, fulled them using a traditional country-style method of stringing them onto a bamboo "bow," and wove them on a bow loom to create a 13-inch-wide cotton fabric known in Korean as *mokmyun* or *mumyong* (no pattern). My mother helped me to "iron" the twelve yards of bumpy-textured, black-dyed cotton by pounding it all night with four mallets, one in each of our hands, until the surface was as smooth and shiny as silk satin. Afterward, she made me a smart new school uniform comprising a white traditional jacket (*chogori*) and a black skirt (*chima*) from the fabric I had woven, and she whispered to me that I would surely become the popular and talented bride of the first son from an important family, an exalted aspiration for any young Korean girl.

Young teaching a student at her International Embroidery School in Korea during the late 1960s.

Opposite:
Roundel depicting domestic silk production (Chinese, Qing dynasty, 1644–1911). This lively scene, embroidered in simple surface-covering stitches in various directions, illustrates the activities associated with domestic silk production. The figures in the foreground and top right are operating bow looms, a traditional type of Chinese loom that produced narrow widths of fabric.

Textiles and needlework carried me from that small Korean village of 30 families along a fascinating pathway across time and geographic region, and I was fortunate to be able to harness this creative medium to positively impact many of my countrywomen's lives. In 1967, at the request of Korea's First Lady and through the auspices of the Ministry of Social Work, I established Korea's first vocational embroidery center, The Women's Center. Located directly across the street from the Seoul train station, this training center taught a marketable skill to some of the young women from the countryside who were streaming into the city each day during this economically difficult period of reconstruction after the Korean War. That year I was commissioned to produce large decorative

Unity, Young's ten-panel screen, in the reception hall of the presidential mansion. The late President Park Jung-Hee (second from right) and his wife, the late First Lady Yook Young-Soo (far left) entertain dignitaries from Germany in the 1960s.

screens representing the theme of "unification" for the Korean presidential mansion (see pages 72–73 and 154–155 for full views) and was invited to present an embroidery exhibition at the prestigious Ikenobo Women's Finishing School in Japan, where I exhibited my own work along with that of students from The Women's Center as well as my own institute, The International Embroidery School, which I had founded in 1965. When I announced that I would donate the entrance fee proceeds to buy embroidery supplies for schools teaching handicapped children in Tokyo, the exhibition was extended from two weeks to three months, I was interviewed by NHK National TV, and I received numerous accolades from the Japanese government, developments that certainly elevated my young embroiderer's spirits. This recognition opened a valuable route for marketing the works created by my students, and their "Handmade Embroidered Handkerchiefs" began to be sold at upscale Japanese department stores such as Takashimaya and Seibu for $5 each, an impressive price in 1967.

The next year, Korean national television produced a documentary that highlighted women of achievement, and based on my work created with a one-inch needle and homemade silk thread, I was featured among the most successful young (under 30) women in Korea in the segment "New Directions in Education." This film recorded the entire process involved in creating a work of embroidery, from drawing the design to mounting the finished piece, and such publicity opened doors that allowed me to introduce new stylistic ideas and economic opportunities to Korean embroidery students.

The story of my work with needle and thread spread internationally, and soon I received invitations to visit Central Asia, North Africa, and the United States to promote

Korean embroidery. An invitation from the Iranian royal court in 1969 provided me with the chance to study carpet-making, and a visit to Cairo, Egypt, resulted in the opening of this market for my student's products, which Seoul newspapers and magazines reported as being the first South Korean items to be sold in a socialist country. The trip to Egypt opened my eyes to the artistic traditions of that ancient land, and I started to create patterns with Egyptian motifs for the handkerchiefs my students embroidered for export to Japan.

In the late 1960s, I began exporting embroidered peasant blouses to the United States, another significant employment opportunity for my students. The American retailers May D&F, Stewart Co., and Lord and Taylor invited me to the United States to exhibit Korean embroidery, and through this I was featured on a CBS television broadcast. As a result, I was asked to present an exhibition at Avanti Gallery in New York, and eventually decided to remain in the United States to pursue graduate degrees at New

Young, wearing a traditional Maio costume, with Maio embroiderers from Gueizho in southern China.

York University. I quickly realized the extent of the West's lack of exposure to East Asian embroidery, and I decided that by studying the history of embroidery technique through the textile study room at The Metropolitan Museum of Art with the late Jean Mailey and by researching the development and spread of this art form, I could deepen my own understanding of embroidery and enhance public appreciation of the subject. My Ph.D. dissertation, "The Origins and Historical Development of Embroidery of China, Japan, and Korea," was, at its publication, the first in-depth, comprehensive study of this topic, and my first book, *The Art of Oriental Embroidery,* became the first English-language reference devoted exclusively to this subject when it was released in 1979. Thus, small needles and

The professional embroiderer with Young learned his craft from one of the descendents of the original founders of his embroidery village, near Hanoi in Vietnam, which was established in the 17th century. He is using the traditional method of stretching the fabric with cord.

homespun silk threads proved to be powerful, life-changing tools that provided me and other Korean women with a viable vocation as well as an expressive and rewarding creative outlet.

Attending the first international Chinese textile conference, held in Hong Kong in 1995, and participating in the study trip to China that accompanied the conference were momentous events in my career. This visit to China offered the opportunity to learn from and share research data with leading Chinese experts in the field, including Dr. Wang Xu, who had supervised the historic excavation of textiles from Han tombs at Changsha in the early 1970s. Dr. Wang Xu's archaeological work had brought to light magnificent examples of chain-stitch embroidery dating to a very early period in Chinese history, and his discoveries had greatly impacted my own understanding of the universality of the embroiderer's art. I realized, too, that the chain stitch and French knots I had learned in the "French embroidery" classes of my childhood were not exclusively French, they were part of a far more ancient tradition that extended across time and place. In another way, the conference in Hong Kong proved to be a great revelation for me: during my long years of working on this topic alone, believing no one else shared my passion, I never dreamed that I would sit down with more than 200 textile experts, students, and aficionados from around the world to discuss and debate the various aspects of woven and embroidered silk down to the last thread.

Harry N. Abrams has kindly invited me to contribute new writing on East Asian embroidery techniques, and it is my greatest pleasure to enhance worldwide understanding of this art by offering technical instruction that space limitations prevented me from including in *The Art of Oriental Embroidery*. I have made numerous visits to East Asia since the publication of that volume, and by examining outstanding works housed in museums and private collections and meeting with experts in the field, I have accumulated valuable information and untold stories on the techniques and materials used in traditional Asian embroidery that will prove beneficial to scholars and practitioners of embroidery alike.

In compiling *Painting with a Needle,* I have invited several embroidery artists with whom I have been associated during my long career to create works in the tradition of East Asia's master embroiderers. These guest artists come from China (including Hong Kong), Korea, and the United States, and represent different levels of skill and various professional backgrounds. Their work includes new designs and ideas taken from the natural environment as well as patterns adopted from earlier masterpieces created by the author.

The projects I have included here for readers to undertake on their own can be created with easily obtainable materials using the simplest methods and are illustrated with my own diagrams. The methods of copying master works, as well as the patterns, instructions, and line drawings, will enable even beginners to create visually compelling examples of embroidery in the East Asian style. As with any art form, once the basics have been thoroughly assimilated, one can freely experiment and create one's own individual style, looking to the natural world and examples from the past for inspiration. The reader will also find here a history of silk embroidery and an overview of selected outstanding historical masterworks from East Asia and Europe that analyzes the stitchery techniques and materials in each piece. By developing a visual familiarity with these masterpieces, readers will be able to recognize the methods seen on works in public collections, distinguish between the various styles and techniques, and gain insight into the aesthetic preferences and artistic intentions of master embroiderers.

It is my heartfelt wish that readers will be inspired to pick up simple left-over household items such as fabric, needle, and thread and with these basic tools create a unique work of art and in so doing experience the creative exhilaration that I have found through "painting with a needle."

Young Yang Chung, 2002

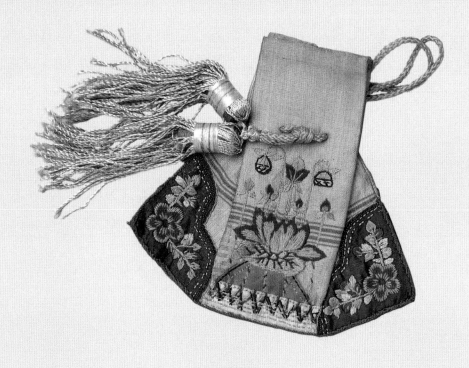

INTRODUCTION

Embroidery ranks among the oldest art forms and remains one of the most enduring means of human expression. In the East Asian region—Korea, China, and Japan—the long history of embroidery and its inseparable link with the progress of early cultures render the chronological study of this craft and its techniques nothing less than a survey of the advent and development of East Asian civilization itself. Fine needles have been discovered at archaeological sites in China dating to as early as 40,000 BC, suggesting that prehistoric peoples could have begun to apply ornament with needle and thread from an extremely early period (see bone needles, right). Sewing seems to have been well developed in the culture of Upper Paleolithic peoples, a time when hunters and fishermen were highly adept at various tool-making techniques as well as grinding, drilling, and polishing. R. J. Forbes has pointed out "Sewing, darning and binding seem well established in Paleolithic times and it has also become very probable from the evidence that the secret of spinning, the trick of twisting fibers into a thread, may have been discovered at this Paleolithic stage."[1]

While the invention of needlework doubtless arose from practical necessity, in Asia the art of stitchery seems to have quickly transcended its utilitarian function to become a powerful vehicle for the expression of aesthetic and sociological ideals. Throughout history, humans have sought to heighten their existence on earth by beautifying the objects around them, and the art of embroidery has long played an important role in this regard. Often referred to euphemistically as "painting with a needle," embroidery allows direct, visual expression of human desires, hopes, and ideals by means of aesthetically pleasing patterns. The uniquely East Asian approach to embroidery has been described as follows:

> Even though embroidery is a decorative art, the Oriental approach to composition was painterly. That is, it strove for artistic realism within the two-dimensional limitations of the medium. Artistic realism, however, is not the same thing as photographic realism: the Oriental artist, whether in embroidery, painting, or any other art form, was never willing to sacrifice artistic effect for mere naturalism, and as far as he or she was concerned, stylization fitted very nicely into this plan. Very often the effect achieved was evocatively beautiful, the truly naturalistic expression of a scene, subject, mood, or idea. This magnificent "painting with the needle" has never been quite paralleled in the history of the textile arts.[2]

Textiles are perhaps the most fragile of all media, and the lack of surviving examples greatly obscures present understanding of the historical development of world fiber arts. Nevertheless, archaeological discoveries in China during the 20th century contributed significantly to our knowledge of the history of embroidery and the roles that

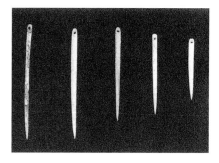

this art form played in early Chinese material culture. Bronzes cast during the Shang dynasty (1600–1027 BC) were sometimes wrapped with silks before being interred in tombs, and although the delicate textiles disintegrated millennia ago, imprints of these silks can sometimes be discerned in the patina of excavated bronzes. Examination of such "ghost silks" sheds light on the weaving techniques practiced in Shang China and suggests that Shang embroiderers might have decorated these fabrics with the earliest straight-covering (satin) stitches. Some early designs remained in the East Asian ornamental vocabulary for a remarkably long period. The powerful thunder pattern and sawtoothlike motifs seen on early bronzes (page 16) and ceramics can still be observed on much later ceramics and textiles.

Among the most spectacular Chinese archaeological discoveries of the late 20th century was that of the fourth-century BC tomb at Mashan, which included a number of magnificently woven and embroidered silks (see opposite). At the time of the burial, this area was part of the kingdom of Chu, a region noted for the excellent quality of its artistic production, particularly in textiles. The Mashan silks reveal the transformation of early Shang geometric designs into more graceful, sinuous patterns. The chain-stitch technique, perhaps derived from finger-manipulated methods of weaving fishing nets, allowed embroiderers to produce curvilinear designs that would have been impossible to achieve using the straight-covering stitches common during the Shang dynasty. Variations in the rendering of the decorative motifs on the Mashan textiles, with some areas more skillfully worked than others, reveal that they were produced as a team effort, with many embroiderers working simultaneously to bring to life designs that had been painted or drawn on the fabric surface with red pigment.

Another stunning archaeological discovery was that of a noblewoman's burial at Mawangdui, a tomb dated to the Western Han dynasty (206–9 BC). Although this tomb probably dates to within a hundred years after the Mashan burial, the textiles found there reveal a significant stylistic shift. The scrolling lines and sweeping volutes of the "Han cloud" designs seen on the Mawangdui silks (page 14) are far more evocative of nature, of the heavenly abodes of the immortals, than are those of the Mashan silks. Clouds were perceived as exceedingly good omens during the Han and remained one of the most continuously invoked auspicious symbols in East Asian art.

Buddhism was introduced into China during the late Han period, and the sophisticated material culture surrounding this new religion provided a tremendous stimulus to Chinese art in all media, particularly with the adoption and promotion of Buddhism at the Chinese imperial court from the Northern Wei dynasty (386–535) through the Tang (618–907) dynasty. With the creation of embroidered images of the Buddha and narrative silk banners, artistic innovations in painting that had developed through the Five Dynasties period (907–967) began to be translated into decorative stitchery, heralding a vibrant new era in the history of embroidery that would culminate during the Song dynasty (960–1279). As seen in a fragment of a Buddhist banner (page 21), Buddhist-themed figural scenes were usually rendered using practical embroidery techniques such

Dancing Phoenix, detail of a quilt (Chinese, contemporary reconstruction of fourth-century BC original excavated from Mashan Tomb 1). Mashan Tomb 1, excavated in the 1980s and dating to the Warring States period, contained a large number of well-preserved textiles, many of which display magnificent decorative patterns in chain stitch. Stylized birds among tendrils, as seen in this example, represent the most widely encountered motif among the Mashan silks. This reconstruction embroidered by a team of Chinese embroiderers and supervised by Wang Yarong and Wang Xu. Authenticated by the Jingzhou Museum in Jiangling, Hubei province.

as simple covering (satin) stitches and chain stitch. Nevertheless, the textured chain stitch was gradually superseded by smooth surface stitches in an effort to create ever more realistic effects. Using the latter technique, decorative patterns were created by covering the fabric according to the desired pattern with straight stitches of various lengths. Large areas could be conveniently filled with very long stitches, on top of which were sewn shorter stitches that not only secured the longer ones but also provided decorative details or supplemental patterns within the individual motifs. These stitches are called decorative stitches. This new type of embroidery, which combined smooth satin covering stitches with these decorative stitches, often creating patterns within patterns, allowed great precision in the rendering of pictorial compositions. Other decorative techniques, such as the long and short stitch, began to be used for shading to create perspective effects. Examples of this technique can be found in costumes, in Buddhist sutra covers created in the Gu style, and in Japanese embroidery. Paintings by great masters began to be copied in needle and thread by skilled embroiderers at the imperial workshops, stimulating demand for this type of artwork among the prosperous gentry.

The Song dynasty can be divided into two distinct periods: the Northern Song (960–1127) and the Southern Song (1128–1279). Military conflict with the Jin Tartars, a nomadic people from northern Manchuria, resulted in the collapse of the Northern Song in 1127 and a 152-year partition of China into northern and southern states. As millions of Chinese fled to the south to escape the northern invasions, the urban centers of the relatively underdeveloped south expanded dramatically. The level of wealth increased, large numbers of new commercial products came onto the market, and Chinese culture in general enjoyed a great flowering. The textile arts flourished along with

Opposite:
Two Hunters on a Hill, album leaf (Chinese, Gu-style embroidery). This masterfully embroidered piece typifies the highly naturalistic style of embroidery pioneered by the Gu family. This piece depicts mounted hunters in Mongolian dress on a hillside, and the saddles are delicately embroidered in decorative stitches. Lively, idealized hunting scenes have remained popular in Chinese art since the Han dynasty, and can be seen in the pictorial tapestries (*kesi*) and album leaves produced during the Song and Ming dynasties.

Above:
Buddhist Banner, fragment (Chinese, fifth century). This embroidered banner, discovered in a cave at Dunhuang in northwestern China, depicts the Buddha on a lotus throne flanked by Xianbei donors of the Northern Wei dynasty embroidered in chain stitch. Eleven stitches were used per centimeter on the donors, shown here. Their clothing is typical of that worn by the Xianbei elite, an ethnic group who ruled this area in the early fifth century.

the economy, and embroidery attained unprecedented heights of technical accomplishment as well as a new fluidity of design. Although embroidery did not become highly commercialized during the Northern Song dynasty, works began to be mass-produced by trained craftsmen at the embroidery workshops of the palace during the Southern Song.

Art was very much a part of the domestic life of the gentry, and Daoism, which was enthusiastically embraced by Southern Song society, was a great influence on both its painting and embroidery: "A combination of these Taoist and Confucian elements was important in the development of landscape painting. . . . Much has been said about Taoism, nature, and landscape; but it seems more and more true to say that the first important, all-embracing philosophy of nature which could lead to a landscape school was . . . the developing Neo-Confucianism of the Song Dynasty."[3] During the Southern Song, professional embroiderers were commissioned to produce compositions that resembled the paintings created by professional artists for gentry households. This type of work is known to us today as embroidery painting—stitching that imitates paintings by the great masters. Embroidery was sometimes even integrated into ink-wash paintings. Most paintings were executed on silk, and the two techniques worked so well together that they were often difficult to distinguish. *Two Hunters on a Hill* (page 20) can be viewed as both a painting and a needlework tapestry. The figures are embroidered in vertical surface satin stitch, and the saddles are embellished in decorative stitches applied on top of the previously made satin stitches, which serves to secure these long stitches and enhance the texture of the saddles. The blades of grass are stitched over painted patterns in order to achieve maximum realism, but to the casual observer it is difficult to tell these two techniques apart. Despite the mysticism and evocative beauty that rendered Song painting among the greatest in Chinese history, embroidery remained a dynamic, independent art form and never became a mere subdiscipline of painting. In fact, Chinese painters and embroiderers seem to have mutually inspired each other from this time onwards. Emperor Song Huizong's enthusiasm for art and his successor's establishment of an embroidery studio within the palace served to train accomplished embroiderers to produce embroidery paintings and to ensure that these technical skills would be passed on to subsequent generations. Song emperors continued to rule southern China until the Mongol onslaught of 1279, when Kublai Khan finally overcame the Song empire and established the short-lived Yuan dynasty (1279–1368).

A much-published Yuan hanging at The Metropolitan Museum of Art in New York provides an example of the methods for filling large surface areas with patterning stitches as perfected during the Song. Entitled *Welcoming Spring*, this magnificently embroidered composition likely decorated a palace wall during seasonal festivities. The mat stitch technique seen on the rocks, mountains, and child's robe, as well as the outline stitch used to define the curly hair on the goats, was probably inherited from Song-style techniques. A similar composition and techniques can be seen on a letter pouch featuring three goats embroidered in decorative stitches (opposite). The bodies of the goats are rendered in long satin stitches, and on top of these are applied short outline stitches

Letter Pouch, detail (Chinese, Qing dynasty, 1644–1911). The Gu style of highly naturalistic embroidery cast an influence on Chinese stitchery, as evidenced by this exquisitely ornamented silk carrier for letters and documents. The scene shown here, measuring 5 by 6 inches, depicts goats and birds in a colorful pastoral setting, with the details rendered in outline stitch over satin stitch, making curls on the fur.

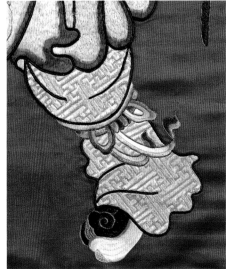

to secure the long stitches and create patterns. This tradition of creating a pattern within a pattern is continued in many contemporary works, such as temple banners and home accessories. An elaborate Daoist banner (opposite) displays at least seven different decorative stitches. An expertly rendered mat stitch is used to articulate the neck of the crane at the foot of the deity (above left), whose trousers are magnificently embroidered with long stitches secured with decorative stitches to create a pattern identical to loom-made damask. To achieve this effect, the entire area of the pant leg was first covered in long horizontal satin stitches, and then short outline stitches were stitched on top of these in the shape of *man* (swastika) characters to imitate a woven pattern (above right). This type of decorative stitchery was popular in the Ming dynasty, and became highly developed during the Qing. Decorative stitches were also used to great effect in Korean and Japanese embroidery. A ten-panel screen (page 28) shows square bookcases that are embroidered in mat and straight satin stitches and are highlighted with delicate decorative stitches to imitate woven fabrics.

The Song tradition of embroidering in a realistic manner that imitated painting continued to exert a great impact on both the embroidery and *kesi* (slit tapestry) weavings of the Ming (1368–1644), Qing (1644–1911), and modern periods. The Gu school of embroidery perfectly illustrates the continuation of Song techniques and refined artistry into later periods. The Gu style, famed for its delicate stitchery and precise rendering of

painterly images, began in Shanghai in the late Ming dynasty with the family of Han
Xi-Meng. This new way of embroidering, which sought to achieve the highest degree of
realism, was pioneered by the Gu school and spread from China to neighboring East Asian
countries. A copy of a Gu embroidery illustrates the characteristic Gu-style techniques
(above). The deer are embroidered in simple surface stitches with exacting detail, using
thin, hairlike threads that fully capture the visual effect of the real animal's fur. The rocks
and grasses were painted onto the fabric before the stitches were added. One of the
author's own works (detail at left) was created as an experiment with the Gu-style techniques. The deer are realistically rendered using fine threads as thin as hairs (eight filaments
twisted into one thread), and some areas, such as the flank, belly, and underpart of the
neck, are blended in two shades using long and short stitches. Long covering stitches are
secured with smaller stitches that provide patterning details such as spots on the body.

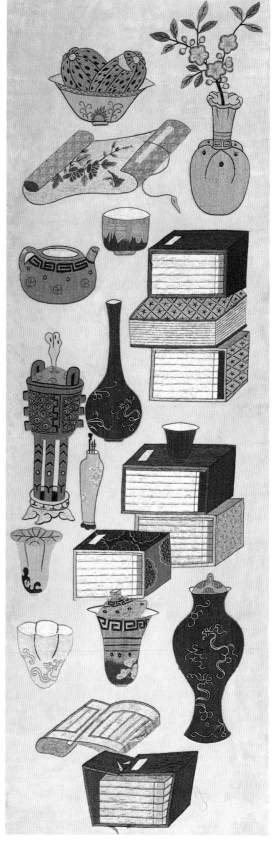

Opposite:

Ten-Panel Screen depicting scholars' objects, detail (Korean, Choson dynasty, 1392–1910). Among the most popular themes for the decoration of men's quarters were the accoutrements typically used by Confucian scholars, such as books, scrolls, pens, and vases. The objects on this early 19th-century screen were articulated with long flat stitches that cover the entire area of the pattern; the shorter stitches applied over these provide the decorative details. For example, the book covers in the two panels are embroidered with laid work (or pattern within a pattern), which is couched down to create patterns imitating silk damask.

Right:

Ten-Panel Screen depicting birds and rocks, detail (Chinese, Qing dynasty, 1644–1911). The landscape elements seen in these two panels were first painted onto the ground fabric. The flowers and birds were embroidered onto the painting in the manner of embroidery painting. Both sides of the screen are decorated, with the opposite side featuring a calligraphic inscription.

The Gu style of embroidery painting soon began to spread across East Asia. Korean and Japanese embroiderers began to work with master designs prepared by professionals painters. The piece at right depicts an eleven-headed Avalokitesvara, which was embroidered over a painted pattern. While the body has been completely covered with stitchery, much of the painting remains visible in the halo area, where only minimal embroidery has been applied. The heads of the bodhisattva are rendered in satin stitch to achieve maximum sheen and smoothness. A skillful combination of painting and embroidery can also be seen in the Gu-style composition on page 32. In contrast to the Avalokitesvara, a realistic surface effect on this piece is achieved by leaving the grassy area unstitched. A skillful combination of embroidery and painting is illustrated in a relatively recent work dating to the late Qing dynasty (page 29). The peony and cherry blossoms on the right panel are embroidered in satin as well as long and short blending stitches. The tails of the wild birds are embroidered in conventional feathery stitches and highlighted with decorative stitchery, whereas the rock formations on both panels and the horizontal lines of the grasses are enhanced by painting with pigments on the ground fabric. This combination of decorative techniques is commonly encountered in East Asian embroidery.

However, throughout history, different regions within China have developed their own regional characteristics. Traditional Chinese silk embroidery can be divided geographically, with the major embroidery centers located in Zhejiang (Suzhou), Sichuan, Hunan, and Guangdong provinces. In addition to these schools, minority peoples in southern China such as the Miao produce embroidery in their own distinctive styles using no patterns and utilizing practical techniques such as counted, cross, and brick stitches in traditional methods and materials.

Aspirations and ideas can be expressed quite literally through motifs and colors in East Asian silk embroidery. The ornamental vocabulary and color schemes used by East Asian artists are replete with symbolism, and this lexicon of design provides embroiderers with an extremely rich cache of building blocks with which to create their own individual patterns. The design seen on page 33 can certainly be appreciated aesthetically without knowledge of its symbolic intent, but its motifs give it profound meaning and purpose as a wedding banner. The "double happiness" character in the center, the dragon and phoenix patterns, and the background color of auspicious red all represent blessings for a newly married couple, while the gourds, peaches, and bats surrounding the central motifs symbolize fertility and good fortune. Textiles created for use during all the rituals and ceremonies that mark the passages and transitions in life—weddings, birthdays, and seasonal festivities—can be similarly arrayed with such auspicious patterns. For instance, the dowry items made by a bride for presentation to her new parents-in-law were often embroidered with cranes, deer, pine trees, and turtles, which were longevity symbols that expressed her wishes for the long life of her mother- and father-in-law. Such motifs can also be seen on spoon cases and on purses (page 15, top), the types of items that would have been traditionally given to elders on their sixtieth birthday.

Eleven-Headed Avalokitesvara (Korean, 20th century). This panel, embroidered by the author in the 1960s, utilizes the Gu-style combination of embroidery and painting to depict a revered eighth-century stone carving of the bodhisattva Avalokitesvara from Korea's Sokkuram Grotto.

Overleaf left:
Album Leaf (Chinese). This Gu-style album leaf depicts a moment in the life of an idealized scholar or official, the natural elements of the setting as well as the facial features and costumes of the human figures rendered with the utmost detail. This piece utilizes minimal stitchery, except for the branches emanating from the craggy rock on the top left and foreground right, which use satin stitches to indicate the leaves. The scholar's trousers were embroidered first in long satin stitches, and then decorative stitches in hexagonal shapes were laid on top.

Overleaf right:
Wedding Banner (Chinese, Qing dynasty, 1644–1911). This hanging would have been hung in the new couple's room. The doubled Chinese character *xi*, meaning happiness, and the paired dragon and phoenix motifs represent the union of man and woman. The composition is rendered entirely in counted stitch, except for the large characters between the dragons and phoenixes, which are couched with gold thread.

Throughout East Asia, clothing and household items were often colorfully embroidered with symbolic motifs. Certain symbols and colors expressed rank and social status: the yellow color and dragon patterns on the twelve-symbol dragon robe (page 36, top) was reserved for the emperor and might have been worn by a member of his immediate family, while the double-crane pattern on the *hyungbae,* or Korean insignia badge, seen at left, indicated a civil official. A 19th-century portrait at right depicts the well-known calligrapher Kim Jeong-hui, his exalted position at court expressed in the brightly colored double-crane insignia on his robe. Other motifs symbolized auspicious wishes, like the crane roundels, infinity symbols, and bats on the Manchu woman's wedding robe (page 36, bottom). Wrappers and coverings of all kinds were exquisitely embroidered. The *fukusa* (Japanese presentation cloth) on page 37 is decorated with turtles that represent auspicious wishes, while the *bojagi* (Korean wrapping cloth) on page 39 is embroidered with propitious flower motifs. The main body of the *bojagi* is made with large squares of red and blue silk gauze, the combination of these two colors representing the yin-yang duality. Religious items were often particularly lavish in their embroidered ornamentation: the Tibetan temple banner on page 40 features abundant symbolic images of Tantric deities and their vehicles embroidered in conventional covering (satin) stitch enhanced with decorative stitches, while the halo is rendered with couching and secured stitches. A Qing Daoist robe (page 15, bottom) is replete with auspicious symbols rendered in satin and decorative stitches and further embellished with gold couching.

Embroidery was more than just a hobby or a pragmatic domestic activity in East Asia, for embroidered silks constituted a valuable commodity with important economic and political functions. Chinese silks were highly coveted luxury items in Europe from the time of the Roman Empire, and they remained among the most desirable imports from the East. The decorative patterns on Asian silks and porcelains, such as flying cranes with pine trees and sumptuous peony branches with rocks, were adopted by European craftsmen into fashionable chinoiserie motifs during the 17th and 18th centuries. These Asian-inspired patterns decorated clothing, wall hangings, and bedcovers and were rendered in a variety of techniques, including canvas and crewelwork embroidery in which the main motifs were sometimes highlighted with silk thread and rendered with surface stitches in a combination of techniques.

While canvas embroidery was commonly used on practical household accessories in Europe, in China the similar tent stitch on silk gauze was used on imperial summer dragon robes, which featured dragon medallions embroidered with gold couching (page 76). Ceremonial robes for government and religious leaders were embellished with impressive gold-couched designs in Europe as well as in East Asia. While the couching technique had been practiced since ancient times, couching with gold thread, a potent symbol of power and wealth in dynastic East Asia, was not introduced in the East until centuries later during the Tang dynasty (618–907). Silk thread wrapped in gilt paper was used to enhance bird and flower embroideries, and gold thread made from gilded animal

Portrait of Kim Jeong-hui (Korean, 19th century). During the Choson dynasty, the court officials wore embroidered insignia badges on the chest and back to indicate the wearer's rank. Double-crane rank badges (seen above and opposite) were worn by first- to third-rank civil officials from the late 18th to the beginning of the 20th century. Embroidered with tightly twisted silk threads, the *hyungbae* features conventional satin stitch on the cranes and horizontal satin stitch on the clouds.

Opposite:
Hyungbae, or rank insignia (Korean, Choson dynasty, 1392–1910).

Top:

Twelve-Symbol Dragon Robe
(Chinese, Qing dynasty, 1644–1911). This dragon robe, embroidered with the twelve authorative symbols and *shou,* or longevity characters, would likely have been worn during birthday celebrations. The blue cloud formations are rendered in satin stitch, the dragons are couched in gold thread, and the standing water waves at the bottom hem are embroidered in diagonal satin stitches.

Bottom:

Manchu Woman's Birthday Robe
(Chinese, Qing dynasty, 1644–1911). Chinese birthday robes were typically of vibrant red, a color that symbolized happiness, and decorated with cranes (seen in the roundels), which represented long life and celebration. The cranes are rendered in conventional satin stitch, and the vertical water waves in diagonal satin stitch.

Opposite:

Fukusa, or Japanese presentation cloth (Japanese, 19th century). In Japan, gifts were typically covered in cloths for presentation, and these covers were often embellished with auspicious imagery. This piece exemplifies the Japanese preference for minimal embroidery, with much of the ground fabric remaining visible. The clams and clouds utilize decorative stitch techniques, in which internal details are applied over the previous stitchery (pattern within a pattern), the turtles are padded, and the frames of the containers are couched in gold metallic thread.

membranes was sometimes used for the silk weaving as well as needlework. The Tang period witnessed the heyday of international trade along the Silk Road, and luxurious Chinese silks were preeminent among the goods exported by caravans from the cosmopolitan Chinese capital of Changan. Archaeological evidence suggests that gold couching was popularly used to decorate robes and costume accessories by the non-Chinese elite of the Jin (1115–1234) and Yuan dynasties. The practice of embellishing court costumes with elaborately couched gold thread was adopted by the Ming imperial household and flourished through the end of the Qing dynasty in the 20th century. In the Middle Eastern region, costumes and accessories seem to have been embellished with metallic threads from an early period, and this custom likely spread to China from the west. Metallic threads can be used to decorate textiles through a number of techniques that varied across time and geographic region. A lavishly embroidered Ottoman sash (page 41) and tray cover (page 42) are embellished with flat strips of gold thread and wire stitched directly onto a linen ground fabric, and the flower stems are created with thinner gold-wrapped threads applied diagonally in satin stitch. The loose weave of the linen ensures that their metallic wrapping will not fray from the core when stitched through the fabric.

Many of the basic stitchery techniques used in the projects featured in this book have remained in the East Asian embroiderers' technical vocabulary for centuries if not millennia. In the 1920s, Russian archeologists discovered frozen tombs dated to about the third century BC at Pazyryk, and the textiles unearthed in these burials reveal the range of techniques used in the production and ornamentation of textiles at that early time. A silk hanging, imported from China, was decorated with bird and tendril patterns in chain stitch that is identical to that used today. Textiles dating to the Warring States period (475–221 BC), excavated at Noin-Ula in Siberia, reveal that by this time embroiderers were working in seven basic techniques: button hole, chain, knot, couching, counted, and quilting stitches, as well as appliqué. These very same methods have been passed down unchanged to modern embroiderers in both the East and the West (page 43).

Today's embroiderers continue a dynamic artistic legacy that extends back into remote antiquity. This volume examines the techniques, materials, and the artistic output of master embroiderers from China, Japan, and Korea in great detail and then provides 19 how-to projects, suitable for all levels of expertise, that allow readers to create their own works within these illustrious traditions. The examples illustrated and discussed here not only familiarize readers with the primary embroidery techniques used in the East and West but also enhance the appreciation and knowledge of this art form while emphasizing connections across time and geographic region.

Bojagi, or Korean wrapping cloth (Korean, Choson dynasty, 1392–1910). This cloth would have been used to wrap wedding documents. The large center section comprises squares of red and blue gauze sewn back to back, the combination of these two colors symbolizing the yin-yang principles. The polychrome embroidered decoration is confined to the ties attached to the four corners.

Opposite:
Thanka (Mongolian, 19th century). This elaborate Mongolian temple banner is densely embroidered with Tantric Buddhist deities and symbolic imagery.

Right:
Embroidered Sash (Ottoman, late 18th or early 19th century). Ottoman embroidery often featured floral patterns, rendered in elaborate metallic thread and double stitchery. On this example, the border and internal details of the stems and leaves are stitched in gold thread on linen fabric. The use of wire thread stitched directly onto thin fabric is characteristic of Central Asian, Ottoman, and Greek embroidery.

Left:
Tray Cover (Ottoman, late 19th century). This elaborately orna-mented tray cover provides a fine example of metallic thread embroidery on thin silk fabric. The vines and leaves are stitched in wire and then couched down to secure the inflexible wire.

Opposite:
Blue Peacock Badge (Korean, 20th century). Many of the traditional Asian silk-embroidery techniques explored in this book are illustrated in this example embroidered by the author in a shape reminiscent of traditional insignia badges. The thunderline patterns in the back-ground are couched in silver thread as a border around the peacock, and the feathers are embroidered in satin stitch in non-overlapping techniques.

OVERVIEW OF STITCHERY TECHNIQUES

STITCHERY TECHNIQUES

The stitches introduced in this chapter form the essential building blocks necessary for the successful completion of the projects in the fourth chapter beginning on page 97. Historical and contemporary examples of each stitch are provided, not only familiarizing new embroiderers with the stitches but also inspiring them with the virtuosity of artists who have used these techniques for centuries.

SATIN STITCH

The satin stitch is a single stitch, sewn in any length or direction—vertically, horizontally, or diagonally—that is repeated as a means of filling space with color or pattern. Perhaps the earliest technique employed by embroiderers, the satin stitch was used in ancient times to embellish garments with symbolic patterns that identified the wearer while beautifying his or her clothing. It remains the most common and universal embroidery stitch.

Previous pages, left:
Standing Water Waves, detail of a wedding robe (Chinese, late Qing dynasty, 1644–1911). During the Qing dynasty, Han Chinese brides typically wore red silk robes abundantly ornamented with auspicious symbols. The five-colored *li-shui,* or "standing water" waves that form the lower border of the robe, are embroidered in satin stitch in the diagonal direction, over padded edging. Each individual line of the water waves is divided into six sections and filled in with four or five shades of the same color stitched in subtle gradation. By examining these water waves, the time period during which the piece was produced can be determined. During the Qing dynasty, embroiderers gradually transformed water waves from curvy to straight while steadily increasing their length. By the late Qing, water waves occupied the full bottom third of dragon robes.

Previous pages, right top:
Dragon Roundel, see caption, page 68

Previous pages, right bottom:
Wedding Robe (Chinese, Qing dynasty, 1644–1911). Twelve dragon motifs are embroidered in gold-thread couching (page 66).

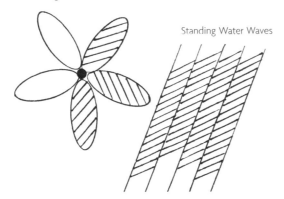

Diagonal Satin Stitch

Standing Water Waves

Above:
Chrysanthemums, detail of a Japanese *obi* (20th century). This detail from a Japanese *obi,* embroidered in the late 1970s by the author for her daughter's wedding, shows chrysanthemum petals embroidered with slanting satin stitches. The petals are rendered leaving a tiny space between each to expose the ground fabric, which helps emphasize the individual shapes of the petals. Each petal is embroidered from right to left, starting at the top (or outer edge) and working toward the bottom (or inner area). Technically, this work characterizes the traditional Japanese style of minimal stitchery: flower seeds are only suggested with a line of dark red thread, the stamens are couched with the thinnest gold thread, and the ground fabric is left exposed on the leaves.

Opposite:
Seven Jewels, detail of a Chinese chair cover (Ming dynasty, 1368–1644). On festive and formal occasions, chairs and tables were often draped with colorfully patterned silk covers. This chair cover would have been used in a wealthy Chinese household during the Lantern Festival, one of the most joyous celebrations of the Chinese calendar. To fill the surface area of the jewels in the dish with vibrant color, the embroiderer simply divided each of them into four or five sections and then stitched each area with straight satin stitch. The coins in between the jewels are also rendered in satin stitch and highlighted with gold couching around the contours. The various motifs on the bowl are embroidered in straight satin stitch as well, which often resembles mat stitch. The base of the bowl is couched with threads wrapped in peacock feathers.

Opposite:

Hyungbae (Korean, 19th century). The rank insignia worn on the front and back of court officials' robes in late dynastic China and Korea are some of the most spectacular examples of embroidery that survive from this period. Bird and animal motifs identified the wearer's rank and position at the Ming and Qing courts in China and the Choson court in Korea. Single leopard patterns designated military officials of the fourth to ninth rank in 19th-century Korea, while the top three ranks were represented by double leopards. Both leopards and tigers, animals that symbolized protection from evil, were used in Korea.

The badges worn by court officials of Korea's Choson dynasty were embroidered in various satin stitches. The body of the leopard was first embroidered with white thread in diagonal satin stitches of irregular length, which were then secured by embroidering the clover-shaped black spots on top of them. The leopard's belly, stitched after the rest of the body had been completed, was embroidered with thinner threads using satin stitches of alternating lengths to create a feathery texture. The eyebrows were embroidered with outline stitches (page 60) in a fan-shaped arrangement, and the whiskers were completed last using threads couched with hidden stitches.

Left:

Ancient Musical Instruments, detail of a ten-panel screen (Korean, 20th century). Musical performances with bronze instruments such as those seen here have for centuries constituted an integral component of Confucian ritual and court ceremony. The straight satin stitches used here, which are irregularly couched down with holding stitches, are used to create a painterly effect. The juxtapositions of the various colors capture the effect of the instruments' metallic surfaces and the aural sensation of the musical tones they produce. The horn and rattle are depicted in straight horizontal stitches secured with vertical satin stitches, a combination that resembles the well stitch (page 65).

COTTON AND THREAD PADDING

Asian embroiderers commonly place various kinds of padding underneath areas to be embroidered to achieve a three-dimensional effect on a flat surface. This padding is then covered over with finishing stitchery such as conventional satin stitches or long and short stitches. Various padding techniques can be observed in a number of historical examples, such as the Daoist robe (page 15, bottom) and the *fukusa* (page 37, turtle at bottom center). The two types of padding utilized in the how-to projects in this book are cotton padding and thread padding, used mainly on the trunks of trees, petals of flowers, and feathers of birds. The embroiderer places a cotton sheet in the middle of the motif and spreads it out in both directions. The thickness of the cotton sheet should be highest in the middle and diminish in both directions as it gets closer to the contours, where a tiny space is usually left just along the inside of the contour. Cotton padding is secured by couching it down at evenly spaced intervals, about 4–5 millimeters apart, in the opposite direction of the finishing stitches, with thread the same color as the finishing stitches. (This helps prevent sinking off, which is when the cotton shows through the finishing stitches.) The couching stitches stop just inside the contours so as not to interfere with any outline stitches. Thread padding is created with tightly packed straight stitches covering the area and sewn in the direction opposite that of the finishing stitches. As with cotton padding, a small space is left between the thread padding and the inside of the contours.

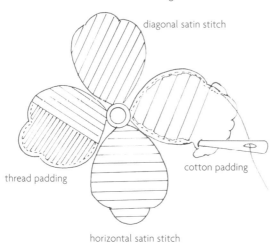

Satin Stitch over Padding

diagonal satin stitch

thread padding

cotton padding

horizontal satin stitch

Left:
Flying Crane, work in progress showing cotton padding.

Opposite:
Three-Panel Screen depicting cherry blossoms, detail (Japanese, 18th century). Perfect examples of the use of heavy padding, the cherry blossoms on this screen are embroidered in long satin stitches over thick cotton-sheet padding. The padding creates the domelike effect particularly noticeable in the center blossom.

Peony, work in progress showing thread padding. This piece illustrates the long and short stitch (page 53) over thread padding. A flowering peony can be created by first defining the contours of the petals with outline stitch (page 60), then filling inside the outlines with thread padding created with straight satin stitch to give the petals a slightly raised, rounded appearance, and finally covering the thread padding and the contour stitches with long and short or satin blending stitches.

Pillow End Pieces (Chinese, Qing dynasty, 1644–1911). These pillow ends are both embroidered over a master design drawn on paper. The long stitches of the lotus leaves appear more full and sumptuous as a result of the paper underpadding.

PAPER PADDING

Paper padding developed as part of a method used by village embroiderers to transfer designs onto fabric, and was particularly useful for closely imitating natural subjects such as birds and flowers. It was a rather primitive way of padding for the villagers, most of whom were not skilled draftsmen. Unlike the custom at palace workshops, which were filled with highly skilled craftspeople and artisans, village embroiderers often shared their ideas as a group and exchanged patterns drawn on paper. These pieces of paper were placed on the fabric, the motifs were stitched through the paper and fabric according to the drawn outlines, and the paper that was not covered by stitchery was torn off, leaving the paper underneath the stitches as padding. The paper padding tradition likely arose as domestic embroiderers felt that they lacked sophisticated draftsmanship skills and sought designs rendered by professionals, but such padding also served to maintain the shape of the designs.

A

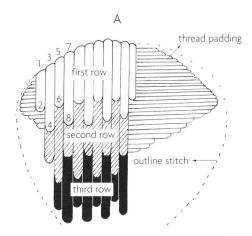

thread padding

1 3 5 7
first row

2 6
4 8
second row

outline stitch

third row

B

hidden stitch

LONG AND SHORT STITCH

While the simple satin stitch covers a space or pattern with a solid block of color, the long and short stitch is used primarily for blending colors within a single motif to heighten its realism. The long and short stitch represents a variation of the satin stitch in which rows of individual stitches alternate in length between long and short in order to modulate color tones and thus achieve shading effects. Gradations of color are created when short stitches of one color from the first row meet long stitches of another color in the next row, and vice versa (diagram A). The meeting points of the long and short stitches are sewn in the "hidden stitch" technique (B), in which the next row of stitches is formed by inserting the needle beneath the stitches in the previous row (pull the thread in the previous row aside with one finger) so that the two rows become meshed or interlocked. A flush meeting of the long and short stitches creates a more harsh transition between colors; be careful not to insert the needle for the second stitch directly on top of the previous one or it will cause the thread of the previous stitch to split.

White Crane, detail of a four-panel screen (Korean, 20th century). Majestic cranes, traditional symbols of long life, have remained a popular motif in East Asian art and embroidery for millennia. This detail of a screen embroidered by the author illustrates the subtle blending of colors that can be achieved with long and short stitches. On the neck, three tones of gray are blended using very thin threads to create a highly naturalistic effect. The scalelike feathers on the crane's back are stitched over thread padding along their contours.

53

Opposite:

White Peacock with Peonies, detail of an eight-panel screen (Korean, 20th century). A passion for peonies, much like the tulip mania that swept 17th-century Holland, spread throughout East Asia during the Tang dynasty. Eventually, peonies came to symbolize wealth, female beauty, and springtime. This sumptuous peony flower, embroidered by the author, is rendered entirely in long and short stitch. Each of the flower petals is created using thread padding under one-third of its surface, and the finishing stitches are made with hand-twisted threads in three tones of red. The rock formation on the left is created with the well stitch (page 65), which leaves the ground fabric partially exposed.

Right:

White Horse, detail (Chinese, 20th century). Horses emerged as a recurring theme in Chinese art during the Han dynasty, when horses became vital to China's military strength and symbolized the power and wealth of the aristocracy. The body of this horse, a detail of a piece by the contemporary Chinese artist Zhao Sui-Ming, is embroidered with irregular satin stitches of dramatically different lengths, while long and short stitches blend the colors on the neck, where the touches of gray seem to have been applied with a painter's brush.

A

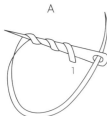

B

C

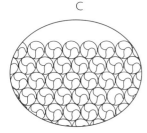

Finished Look

A

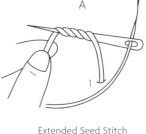

Extended Seed Stitch

B

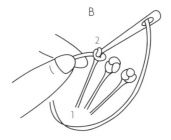

C

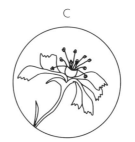

Finished Look

SEED STITCH

The seed stitch, a variation of the knot stitch, is created by wrapping the thread tightly around the needle and holding it taut (diagram A). Insert the needle back into the ground cloth right next to where you came up, hold the needle upright, push the wrapped threads down to the cloth with a finger, then pull the needle through while still holding the threads down so they will be secured properly (B). The seed stitches of the second row and all subsequent rows fit between the stitches of the previous row so that there are no gaps and no ground fabric shows (C). These raised, individual stitches can be arranged in a group or scattered across the fabric and are often used for flower seeds, especially on the stamens of flowers (extended seed stitch), and in areas that require texture (page 53, crane's crown). The extended seed stitch is a slight variation on the seed stitch: after the thread has been wrapped around the needle, insert the needle a slight distance from where you came up. The knot stitch, one of the oldest East Asian embroidery techniques, can be seen on textiles excavated from Chinese Chu tombs dated to the fourth century BC.

Opposite, left:
Key Holder (Chinese, Qing dynasty, 1644–1911). Chinese clothing was constructed without pockets, so personal items were carried in small bags and pouches that hung from a belt. The objects typically used by Confucian scholars, such as the scrolls and vases rendered in seed stitch on this case, were popular decorative patterns on East Asian textiles and screens. In creating these individual seed stitches, the embroiderer wrapped the needle with thread only once to create the tiniest of stitches.

Opposite, right:
Elephant Pendant (Chinese, Qing dynasty, 1644–1911). This pendant is densely embroidered on both sides with more than 100 knots per square centimeter. The stuffed elephant is embellished with jewels rendered in seed stitch on its head and neck, seven hand-twisted tassels across the bottom, and numerous decorative knot stitches on either side. Elephants symbolized strength in Tibetan Buddhism, and such an intricately wrought pendant would have been worn by a lady of great wealth.

SACRED
TO THE MEMORY OF
MRS. *SUSANNAH BREWSTER*,
WHO DEPARTED THIS LIFE,
MARCH 24, 1808.
IN THE 47th YEAR OF
HER AGE.

Opposite:

Memorial Embroidery (American, early 19th century). This type of project was popular in 18th- and 19th-century Britain and America where grieving women sometimes embroidered pictures to commemorate recently deceased loved ones. This memorial embroidery was created by stitching the main symbolic motifs on a painted silk background. The scene features massive seed stitches for the leaves of the tree on the right. The long leaves of the weeping willow are created with feathery satin splinter stitches (page 138) in which darker threads are overlaid on the top of the previously laid stitches to create a three-dimensional effect. The style and technique of this piece, which is signed by the artist, Margaret Brewster, and dated 1808, are typical of the period, but the combination of painting and embroidery shows the Asian influence.

Right:

Peony Medallion (Chinese, late Qing dynasty, 1644–1911). During the hot summer months, upper-class Chinese wore robes made of fine silk gauze, often embroidered with motifs appropriate to the season. While young women chose robes in bright colors, older ladies favored more subdued hues, such as black. The peonies on this medallion taken from a black gauze summer robe are embroidered in four shades of red using seed stitch. The camellias and butterflies are embroidered in counted stitch, also known as brick stitch (page 77).

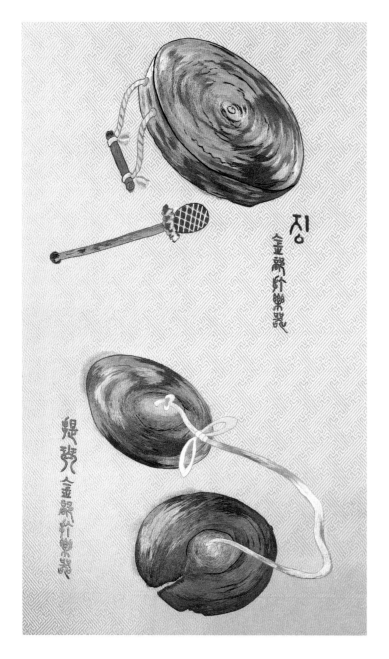

OUTLINE STITCH

This stitch, also known as the stem stitch, represents the most basic technique for creating a line. The outline stitch is used primarily for rendering thin lines and stems, but greater thickness can be obtained by adding stitches to the contour. The latter method is ideal for filling in large curved areas. Diagram A illustrates the thinnest outline width, B demonstrates a medium-width outline, and C shows the thickest form of outline stitch. One of the earliest Chinese embroidery techniques, the outline stitch can be seen on textiles dating to the fourth century BC.

Left:

Gong and Cymbals, detail of a ten-panel screen depicting musical instruments (Korean, 20th century). The striking of gongs and cymbals featured prominently in solemn Confucian rituals as well as more lively popular musical performances. These vibrantly colored Korean instruments, which were embroidered by the author, are completed entirely in outline stitch, which produces a rather painterly effect. In order to achieve a metallic sheen, the large spaces are filled with outline stitch (diagram B) using greens, browns, and beige rather than conventional shading techniques.

Opposite:

Herons, Weeds, and Water Waves, detail of a folding screen (Japanese, 18th century). For centuries, the meeting point of water and land has captured the imagination of artists in Japan, an archipelago with abundant lakes, rivers, and streams. These herons and weeds, and their reflections in water, are all rendered in outline stitches of various widths. The thinnest outline stitch is used along the horizontal lines of the water reflection and the birds' tails; the standing grasses in the foreground are created with medium-width stitches; and the thickest form of outline stitch is used for the curving water in the foreground. The herons themselves are embroidered in diagonal satin stitch with twisted white thread.

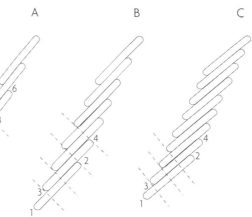

A   B   C

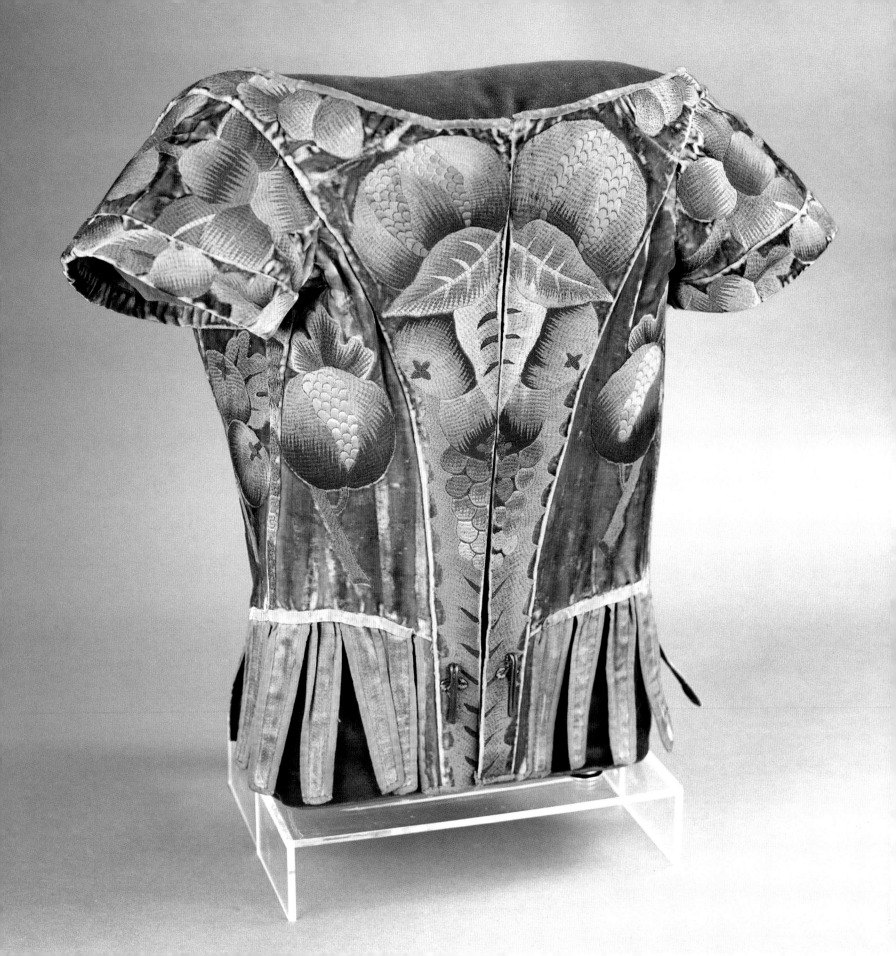

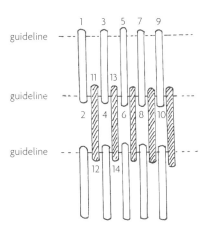

Finished Look

MAT STITCH

The mat stitch is a variation of the vertical satin stitch in which each row is connected with the others in an interlocking framework, which can be densely or sparsely applied. The embroiderer can first stitch guidelines in straight stitch directly on the cloth to help in measuring the length of each row of stitches, then stitch the interlocking vertical rows over the guidelines. The texture of the finished mat stitch is determined by the space between the stitches and the interlocking rows. A tightly applied mat stitch, with no space at all between the stitches, is called "packed" in embroiderer's parlance, and creates a velvety effect. Both European and Asian embroiderers used this stitch to fill up large areas with color and pattern. The durable mat stitch was also popular for rendering Buddhist banners, accessories, and other items that needed to last, such as the rank insignia used in the courts of East Asia. This custom of covering a large area with durable stitchery extended into the Qing dynasty and continues today in the embroidery of works for temples (page 25).

Opposite:
Young Girl's Bodice (Italian, 17th century). European costume was often embellished with intricately embroidered patterns, such as these pomegranates, using techniques similar to those found in East Asia. The mat stitches on this boned bodice are interlocked, or packed without space between them, which gives the surface a velvetlike texture.

Right, top:
Hyungbae, detail (Korean, Choson dynasty, 1392–1910). This detail of a single-crane rank badge, which signified a fourth- to ninth-rank civil official in the 19th century, shows stylized mountain peaks rising from crashing waves (right and left of peaks), images that symbolized all the lands and seas of the earth.

Right, bottom:
Thanka, detail (Tibetan, 16th century). The central blue Buddha, the background behind the Buddha, and the beige figure lying beneath the feet of the blue figure are all rendered in mat stitch.

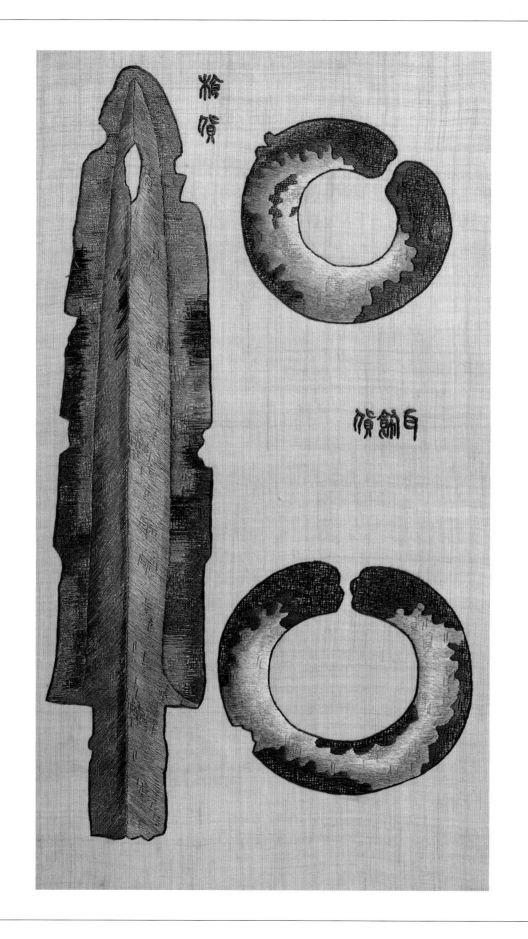

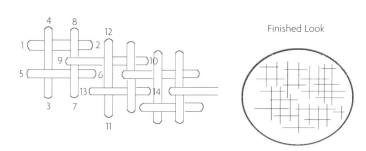

WELL STITCH

The well stitch (named by the author) is convenient for subtly filling in large background areas in such a way that does not compete visually with the stitchery of the main subject. The term "well" stitch is derived from the Chinese character for "water well," which is constructed with four strokes, two horizontal and two vertical, leaving a square in the center.

Finished Look

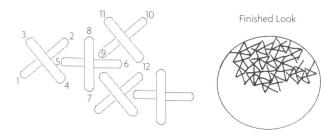

Finished Look

Opposite:
Ancient Copper Coins, detail from a ten-panel screen (Korean, 20th century). These round and dagger-shaped coins were embroidered by the author on unbleached ramie in mat, well, and diagonal satin stitches, a combination of techniques intended to create a three-dimensional effect that evokes the texture of the old coins. For example, the satin stitches on the blade are sewn with lighter-colored threads in a slanting direction to catch the light, while the less glossy well stitches serve as a contrast to the sheen.

STAR-CROSS STITCH

The star-cross stitch (named by the author) is used to fill in large spaces and to create a textured appearance. The technique involves creating a group of individual crosses, each made of two stitches of irregular lengths, one over the other, all crosses touching each other at their points to form a cluster of stitches (see master work page 118).

Above:
Ancient Musical Instruments, detail of a ten-panel screen (Korean, 20th century). Musical instruments like those seen on this screen originated very early in Chinese history, and well-preserved examples have been excavated from Chu tombs dating to the Zhou period (1027–256 BC). The traditional instruments on this screen were created entirely in the well stitch using heavy-twisted threads.

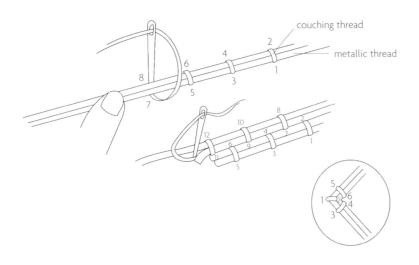

COUCHING STITCH

Couching refers to the securing of "floating" metallic threads onto the surface of fabric with thin silk threads, called couching threads. Silk or paper cord threads wrapped in gold foil are laid on the surface of the fabric to create a pattern, and then "couched" down or held in place with evenly spaced stitches of silk thread. Pairs of metallic threads are usually couched together, and where the design requires areas of densely packed metallic thread, several pairs are lined up together. The couching stitch was invented to prevent gold- and silver-wrapped threads from fraying—embroiderers found that when pierced through fabric, the metal leaf encasing the silk thread

core had a tendency to separate and unravel. It is also more gentle on the delicate silk ground fabric and creates texture.

Practiced in China as early as 475 BC, this technique became extremely popular at the court of the Kangxi emperor (17th century), where it symbolized the political and economic stability resulting from his consolidation of the vast Qing empire. Gold couching was also widespread in Europe about the same time, particularly for ecclesiastical and ceremonial robes. Imperial robes, medallions, and costume accessories worn at the Chinese court were almost invariably embellished with patterns composed of costly gold threads, particularly during the late Qing period.

Above:
Peony, detail of a decorative panel (American, 20th century). In the Chinese language, peonies are often referred to as *fu gui hua,* or "flowers of riches and honor," indicating the high esteem in which they are widely held. This peony is highlighted against a background screen of geometric shapes created with couched gold threads. This work in progress was created as an experiment with couching techniques. Embroidered by Dana Bloch.

Opposite:
Peacock Insignia (Chinese, early Qing dynasty, 1644-1911). The entire background of this magnificent insignia badge, its peacock pattern indicating that it was worn by a third-rank civil official at court, is densely embroidered with gold couching. The brilliant background of this exceptional example is created with gold threads laid down and couched in a wide variety of geometric shapes, from undulating squares and trapezoids to long formations that sail across the face of the fabric like shooting stars. The rock formation and parts of the bird's body are formed with couched threads wrapped in peacock feathers.

Opposite:

Dragon Roundel (Chinese, Qing dynasty, 1644–1911). Metallic threads can be couched to a ground fabric using a number of methods. The desired pattern and the thickness of the metallic threads usually determined the method as well as the color of the couching threads that would be used. This dragon medallion, one of a pair on a robe, provides an example of gold couching without the use of padding underneath the pattern. The individual scales of the dragon, created by layering one scale over the top of the previous one, are couched with red thread in the conventional manner for depicting scales.

Right:

Chasuble (French, 18th century). Richly patterned ecclesiastical vestments have played an important role in the visual culture of Roman Catholicism. This ceremonial chasuble features decorative patterns of undulating ribbons and tulips. The ribbons are embroidered in gold couching with thick metallic threads along the center with dragonfly wings stitched in gold thread on top. The lacy patterns on the ribbons are created by couching down the white silk thread in trailer patterns with gold thread.

Overleaf left:

Rank Insignia (Chinese, late Qing dynasty, 1644-1911). In the chaotic political climate of the late Qing dynasty, when governmental rank could be obtained through purchase or bribe, insignia badges were often created with detachable motifs that could be easily changed with the wearer's rank. This particular badge was made commercially for just such a purpose. All of the decorative patterns on this rank insignia are created with colored metallic-wrapped thread couched with yellow thread.

Overleaf right:

Peacock Roundel (Chinese, Qing dynasty, 1644–1911). This peacock insignia badge is lavishly embroidered in the couching technique with colored cord and gold metallic thread.

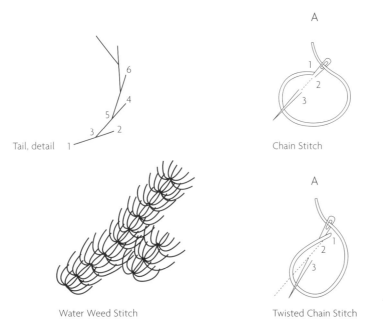

Tail, detail

Water Weed Stitch

A   B   C

Chain Stitch

A   B   C

Twisted Chain Stitch

WATER WEED STITCH

Each element of the feathery water weed is composed of a series of outline stitches, or a variation of the outline stitch, in which wispy "tails" are created for a realistic effect. A center vein can be created with the outline stitch from which the tails emanate, and each tail itself consists of a series of outline stitches stitched in a curving pattern. The tails can also be stitched without the center vein (see Project 18).

CHAIN STITCH

The chain stitch is a technique that connects individual loops to create a line or fill a pattern. Several variants of the chain stitch are practiced worldwide. Examples of chain stitch have been discovered in various tombs in Siberia and East Asia dating to as early as the fourth century BC. Identical chain-stitch techniques can also be found on ancient South American and ancient Egyptian textiles. The chain stitch provides the most convenient method for creating and filling curvilinear patterns. In diagram A the loops are linked to create a line or fill a pattern. To cover curved contours smoothly, an even line can be obtained by pulling the needle at an angle. The twisted chain stitch is textured and raised higher than the other chain-stitch technique.

Previous spread:
Unity, a ten-panel screen depicting swimming fish (Korean, 20th century). The author received the commission for this piece in the 1960s from the South Korean government, which at the time sought to express its desire for the unification of Korean peoples through the visual arts. The author chose to depict a school of fish to express the idea of togetherness. The weeds the fish are swimming through are stitched in the outline technique leaving the tail as part of the pattern.

See page 19:
Dancing Phoenix, detail of a quilt (Chinese, contemporary reconstruction of fourth-century BC original excavated from Mashan Tomb 1). The embroiderers of this time worked almost exclusively in chain stitch and excelled at producing images of gracefully curvilinear dragons, tigers, and fantastical birds, animals that featured prominently in the shamanistic spiritual beliefs of the people of the era. This reconstruction embroidered by a team of Chinese embroiderers and supervised by Wang Yarong and Wang Xu. Authenticated by Jingzhou Museum in Jianling, Hubei province.

Opposite:
Bedcover (India, 17th century). The phoenix, a mythical bird in East Asia, also appears in East Indian embroidery. This bedcover, ornamented entirely in chain stitch, features paired phoenixes on the top and bottom depicted with personifications of the five senses wearing fanciful combinations of European, Indian, and Persian costume.

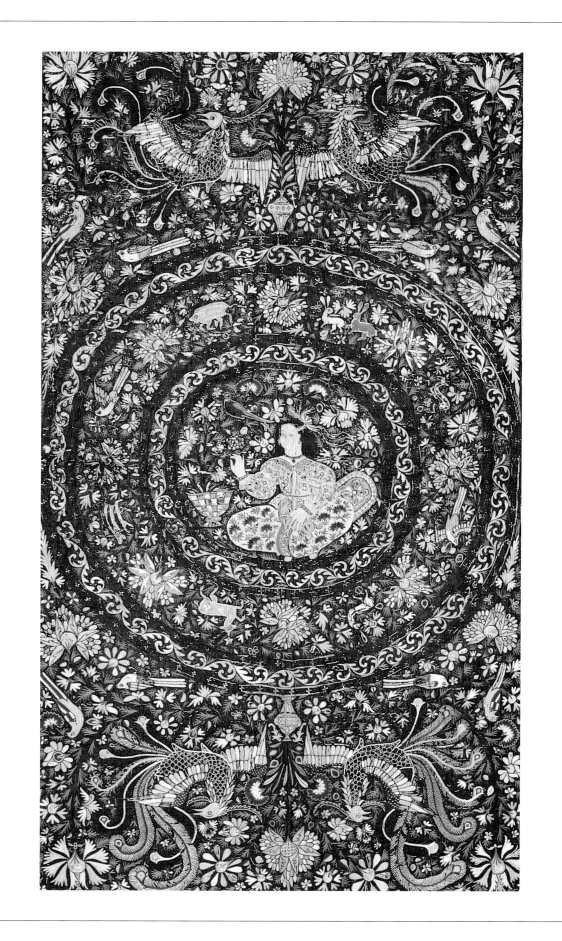

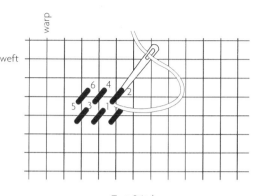

Tent Stitch

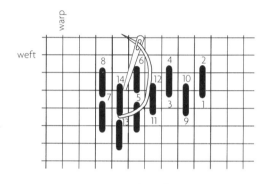

Brick Stitch

Opposite:

Imperial Family Dragon Badge (Chinese, Qing dynasty, 1644–1911). While members of the extended imperial clan wore dragon-patterned insignia badges in the form of a square, a shape that represented the earth, members of the immediate imperial family wore round badges (*po*), a shape that symbolized the universe. The clouds, water waves, and flaming pearls (spheres surrounded by flames) in the background of this 18th-century insignia badge are rendered in brick stitch, while the dragon is couched with metallic thread.

Right:

Pleated Skirt (Chinese, Qing dynasty, 1644–1911). This skirt, a type worn by Chinese aristocrats for ancestral rituals as well as horseback riding, is made of silk gauze embroidered with both counted stitch and gold thread couching. The dragon motifs are created with couched gold metallic threads to glorify the wearer's exalted position, while the secondary symbolic motifs, including the water waves, clouds, and flaming pearls above the dragon heads, are rendered in brick stitch.

COUNTED STITCH

The counted-stitch technique involves the embroidery of short stitches on to an open-weave fabric. Counting the warps (vertical threads in fabric) and securing the stitches onto the warp in a diagonal direction are known as the tent stitch, while affixing stitches to the wefts (horizontal threads in fabric) in a straight (upright) direction is known as the brick stitch. The length of the stitch and the direction in which it is carried determine the character of the pattern.

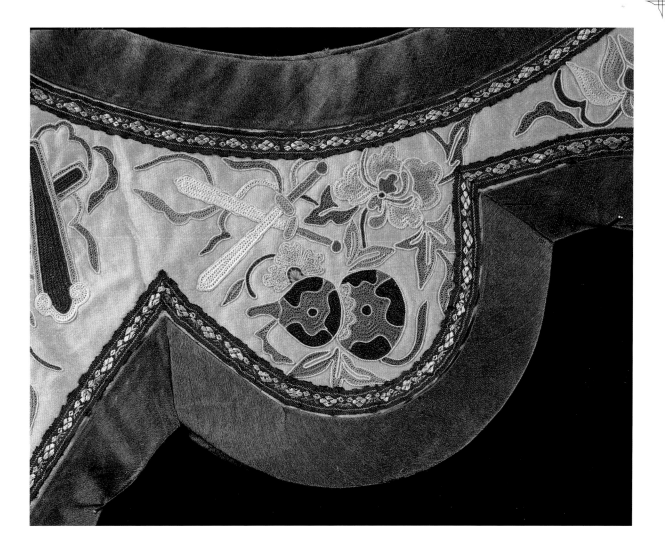

Fan Case and Waist Band Pouch
(Chinese, Qing dynasty, 1644–1911).
This set of accessories for a man
is embroidered in tent stitch.
Both items are stitched with
gold thread to highlight the bat
motifs, symbols of luck and happiness. Since traditional Chinese
costume was constructed with no
pockets, pouches and cases such
as these were attached to the
waistband as a means of carrying
personal belongings.

Right:
Child's Hat, detail (Chinese, Qing
dynasty, 1644–1911). Children's hats
were often made in the shape of
fierce animals to ward off evil spirits, and/or embroidered with auspicious symbols that wished the
wearer long life and good fortune.
This hat is embroidered entirely
with tiny holding-loop stitches.
The use of two needles with
two threads is an intense mental
and technical challenge for the
embroiderer, yet surprisingly it was
utilized for relatively small items.

HOLDING-LOOP STITCH

The Chinese term *wan xiu* literally means
"holding stitch" or "pulling stitch." One
of the most intriguing East Asian embroidery techniques, this stitch requires the
use of two needles at the same time,
one needle making loops and the other
securing them down. The holding-loop
stitch can be used to fill a pattern or to
create decorative lines. The finished
stitchery is so similar in appearance to
the seed stitch that experienced eyes
often cannot distinguish between the two.

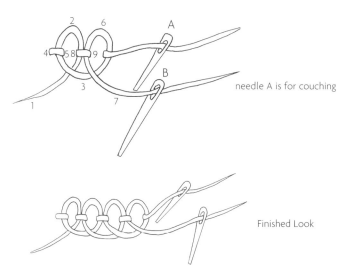

needle A is for couching

Finished Look

Weave Stitch

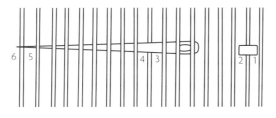

warp

Finished Look

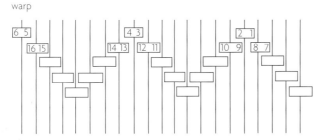

WEAVE STITCH

This painstaking technique requires passing the needle through the warp (vertical) threads of the ground fabric. First, the main points of the pattern are marked on the fabric after counting the warps, and then the needle carries the thread in the weft (horizantal) direction, crossing over the warp where the pattern is desired and passing under the warps in the unpatterned areas. This technique was developed and perfected during the Ming dynasty (1368-1644), when it was employed on small objects worn by the upper class.

BULLION-KNOT STITCH

This stitch is primarily used to create texture, especially in such motifs as tree trunks and branches. The thread is wrapped around the needle five to ten times and the needle goes back down into the fabric at a distance from the point where the needle came up so that the coiled threads lie flat and even and don't bunch up. (See pages 99 and 104 for examples of the bullion-knot stitch.)

Opposite:
Butterfly, detail (Chinese, Qing dynasty, 1644–1911). Beautiful butterflies, traditional symbols of joy and the summer season, represent a favorite subject for Chinese poets and artists. This half of a round decorative plaque from a woman's robe is embroidered entirely in holding-loop stitches with light blue threads starting from the contours and working inwards, leaving out the dots of the eyes.

Right:
Fragrance Pouch (Chinese, Qing dynasty, 1644–1911). In dynastic China, colorfully decorated cloth pouches filled with sweet-smelling herbs and dried flowers were commonly hung from belts and canopy beds. Probably intended as an accessory for a wedding bed, this fragrance pouch features elaborate designs created with weave, counted, and satin stitches.

A   B

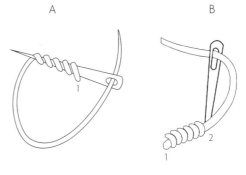

Bullion-Knot Stitch

TOOLS AND MATERIALS — A BRIEF HISTORY

THREADS

Archaeological discoveries indicate that sericulture—the production of silk by raising silkworms—was first practiced during the Shang dynasty (1600–1027 BC). Then, it was a much simpler process than the vast industrial methods used today, but regardless of the methods used, it was and still is the careful, painstaking craft and science of making the silkworm cocoon yield a vast supply of extremely durable silk thread. By today's standards, the old ways of production are quite inefficient, yet high-quality silk was produced from a very early period. The shops where silk was produced were small in the early dynasties, and the work was usually done by women. Sometimes a single operator manipulated thousands of silkworm trays and did all of the steaming and reeling. In other cases, whole families had their own silkworm farms and produced silk for their own use or sold it at the great markets.

Since poor care produced poor silk, the quality of silk was carefully managed by the assiduous sericulture process. Study of the proper climate and the type of soil used in the cultivation of the mulberry trees (whose leaves are the silkworm's favorite food), the proper harvesting of the leaves and their spreading in the silkworm trays, the industrious methods of raising the silkworm cocoon, steaming, reeling, and finally spinning—all of these steps in the process were first conceived and mastered by the Chinese. The

Previous pages, left:
Bamboo spools of peacock-feather-wrapped thread from China.

Previous pages, right top:
Skeins of commercially-twisted silk thread from Korea.

Previous pages, right bottom:
Spools of untwisted silk thread from Japan.

Opposite:
The author at her studio in the 1980s controlling the thread with her left hand while pulling down with the other hand in order to lay the threads evenly.

Right:
Tools and materials for embroidery.

dyeing process was also very important, as improper dyeing could radically affect the strength, tensility, and sheen of the thread.

In the dynastic period, spun silk threads were always twisted by hand in preparation for sewing. Varying thicknesses and, consequently, varying techniques of twisting were required. Hand twisting of the threads allowed greater or less delicacy, according to the shape and size of the design and the artistic effect desired. Hand-twisted threads also lent themselves to greater facility in threading and easier handling of the fabric when sewing. It was found that thick threads required larger needles, which made unsightly, larger holes in the silk, so smaller needles were used and the silk threads were twisted to the same thickness, or slightly less, than the eye of the smaller needle. It was also more effective in terms of finishing; embroidery done with hand-twisted thread had considerably more sheen and uniformity of textural surface. Two-color threads were obtained easily by hand twisting also.

Metallic threads of gold and silver were made by pounding gold or silver stock into leaf, which was then sliced into very narrow strips and rolled or twisted onto the thread. Gold or silver paper, or gold-painted paper, which was more economical, was also used for this purpose. Such threads were always couched on top of the fabric with a securing stitch, since the stitching-through of metal threads could tear the fabric and often caused the gold or silver to fray.

THE ROLLER EMBROIDERY FRAME

In East Asia, the embroidery frame traditionally used in the home and by professionals was square or rectangular, in contrast to the Western embroidery hoop. Although the hoop has been used in the East, the rectangular frame is still preferred today. Round hoops are lighter, easier to handle, and useful on smaller pieces or with cotton or linen, but the rectangular frame offered more advantages such as less wrinkling of the fabric, greater stability, and the easier accommodation of larger pieces of fabric. The clamping and wrinkling caused by a hoop can tear or damage delicate silk, and size is important too, the hoop not being convenient on larger pieces, such as screen panels. As revealed in a number of paintings such as the one on page 90, rectangular frames were probably used exclusively in most of China, Korea, and Japan. The how-to projects in this book, beginning on page 101, are secured to rectangular frames.

FABRICS

Silk weaving in ancient China was preceded by a long history of the production of other fabrics on the bow loom. Animal fibers came from sheep for wool, and goats, camels, and later, horses, for hair fibers. Plant fibers, either stem or bast, were obtained from flax (linen), jute, hemp, and ramie, a plant native to China whose special linenlike bast fiber was very useful in the production of cloth. Felting, an import from Central Asia, was also extensively practiced. Quilted garments for the cold Chinese winters and hemp cloth for summer were produced as early as the Yangshao Painted Pottery cultures (ca. 4000 BC).

Opposite:
The author visiting Suzhou Embroidery Institute in China. She is holding long stretcher side bars used by contemporary embroiderers.

With the discovery and cultivation of silk, the simple bow loom was used to produce a cloth in both tabby and twill weaves. The thickness of weft and warp threads determines the weight and texture of silk, and plain-weave silk was made in many different textures and weights. Oriental silks were traditionally prepared in extra-fine, fine, rough, and extra-rough grades. Generally, silk embroidery threads were used; finer fabric required the use of a finer thread, and heavy silk could take a thicker thread.

Great variety of color may not have been available much before the Han dynasty, but important advances in dyeing during the later Tang and Southern Song dynasties allowed a seemingly endless variety of colors.

Complicated designs usually require a finer grade of fabric and thread. Since silk embroidery is smooth and delicate by nature, rough textures were achieved sometimes through rough fabric, but more characteristically through the preparation of the thread by a special twisting method. A variety of textural effects in such motifs as flowers, rocks, trees, and bird feathers can be obtained through the use of textured thread and stitching techniques.

The draw loom was probably in use in China by the end of the Han dynasty. With its development, other fine silk fabrics, such as warp-patterned, weft-patterned, and

Students at Suzhou Embroidery Institute working on a piece held on a stretcher with side bars similar to those held by the author on page 87.

gauze weaves could be produced, and these lent themselves to innovative embroidery effects. Damasks, a later development, were reversible, warp-faced designs on a weft-faced ground, or vice versa. The word "damask" takes its name from the ancient Near Eastern city of Damascus. Available in various weights and textures, damask is used in the West for tablecloths, drapery, and upholstery, but in the East it was often the ground fabric for beautiful robes and other textiles upon which polychrome embroidery was executed. Brocades have designs inlaid as the weaving progresses. The treatment is found on damasks, twills, satins, or plain-weave silk. Both brocades and damasks were embroidered with the same stitchery that was employed on plain weave, the former simply providing a richer, more varied ground.

NEEDLES

Both the needle and the threads selected had to be appropriate to the thickness of the fabric and the design. East Asian embroiderers used a variety of short, very fine, pinlike embroidery needles in a number of sizes, the average being about one inch long. The eye ends were flattened and had round eyes. Early needles in China were made of bone and ivory (page 17), then copper, bronze, and finally steel, but ivory needles were still found in use there as late as the Qing dynasty. Knotting of the thread end was never done in any Oriental technique, for knots created unsightly bulges and bumps on the surface after the composition had received its backing. Instead of a traditional knot, a top anchor "knot" was executed (page 94).

Embroiderer Kim Tae-Ja working on *White Peacock with Peonies* at her studio.

STARTING AND ENDING METHODS

All of the items mentioned below can be purchased at most embroidery or art supply shops or you may consult the List of Suppliers on page 173.

BASIC DESIGN TRANSFER METHOD

Step 1 For each of the projects beginning on page 101, use a copy machine to copy the design (see line drawing that accompanies each project) from the book page and enlarge it to the desired size.

Step 2 Trace the design onto tracing paper with wash-off pencil.

Step 3 Place carbon paper (dressmaker or wax-free transfer paper) inkside down onto the fabric. (Use light-colored carbon paper on dark fabrics and dark-colored on light fabrics.)

Step 4 Place the tracing paper with design traced on it on top of the carbon paper.

Step 5 Secure the tracing and carbon papers, with straight pins or sew with a temporary stitch or two.

Step 6 Use a ballpoint pen (so as not to tear the tracing paper) to trace the design onto the cloth.

Step 7 Remove the tracing and carbon papers and check the motif. If any lines are weak, fill them in with a washable cloth marker, or stitch with darning stitches.

DESIGN TRANSFER METHOD FROM ANTIQUE PIECES

Step 1 Take a snapshot of the piece with a camera (any camera will do). The photo should be as close up to the piece as possible and sharply focused.

Step 2 Enlarge the snapshot to the desired size using a copy machine.

Step 3 Trace the design onto tracing paper with wash-off pencil and follow Steps 4–7 above.

Previous pages, left:
Reverse Painting (Chinese, Qing dynasty, 1644–1911). These court women in China are transferring a pattern onto the fabric while a courtesan embroiders on a piece that is stretched on a traditional rectangular frame.

Previous pages, right top:
A master embroiderer at Suzhou Embroidery Institute. She is ending a thread and snipping off the excess before she begins a new thread.

Previous pages, right bottom:
Applying glue to a canvas stretcher.

MOUNTING THE FABRIC ON A STRETCHER

Step 1 Buy a commercial, four-sided canvas stretcher and assemble it. To determine the size of stretcher you will need for the projects in this book, take the dimensions provided for each project and add three inches to all sides. The additional three inches gives you room for gluing and pinning the muslin.

Step 2 Transfer the design onto the fabric following the method described on page 92, then sew a muslin border onto two sides of the fabric. Sew a strip of muslin (a few inches to several inches wide) onto the fabric with simple securing stitches about half an inch inside the edge of the fabric. When you need to stretch out the fabric, pull on this muslin border.

Step 3 Glue the two sides of the fabric without a muslin border onto the stretcher, using wallpaper glue and water (page 91, bottom). Apply the glue to the stretcher, not the fabric. For the glue, use commercial wallpaper glue powder mixed with water to a pancake-batter-like consistency, but slightly thicker. It should be softer than gumlike. Make sure about half an inch of the fabric is glued down, and let dry for at least one hour. You can also use pushpins to secure it while the glue dries.

Step 4 Pull the two unglued sides of the fabric (with the muslin border) tighly onto the frame, and then pin them down in two corners with pushpins.

Step 5 Add additional pins all along the four sides of the frame so that all sides are secure.

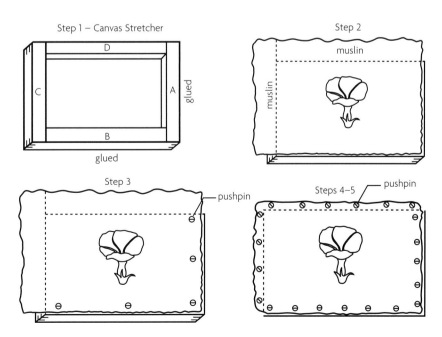

Step 1 – Canvas Stretcher

Step 2

Step 3

Steps 4–5

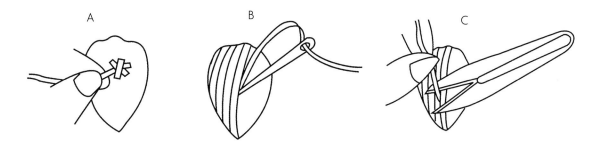

A   B   C

One of the characteristics of silk embroidery is the absence of bulging knots. Instead, the silk embroiderer anchors threads down at both beginning and end, eliminating the need for unsightly knots.

ANCHORING—STARTING AND ENDING A THREAD

Step 1 When starting with a new thread, pierce through the fabric from top to bottom with the needle and pull the thread through, being careful to leave about a two-inch tail.

Step 2 While holding the two-inch tail down with a finger, sew three or four stitches on top of it, making a starlike pattern (diagram A).

Step 3 Proceed with regular embroidery stitches over the tail area.

Step 4 To end a thread, repeat Step 2 (B). Pull the thread taut and snip with scissors (page 91, top, and C, above). Always begin and end a thread beneath previously made stitches.

FINISHING METHOD

Step 1 When the embroidery is completed, dust off the finished work gently using a velvet sponge.

Step 2 Turn the frame over to the back and cut off any remaining loose threads.

Step 3 Secure the stitches by applying a small amount of rice glue to the back of the embroidery on the threads only. Make sure the glue contains all-natural ingredients, otherwise it will ruin the fabric.

Step 4 Steam the finished embroidery with boiling water (see diagram at right). Steam from a tea kettle generally works better than from a pot because the steam is forced out of a small hole in a more concentrated, forceful blast. Steam the back of the embroidery only, never the front—this evens out the surface of the stitches.

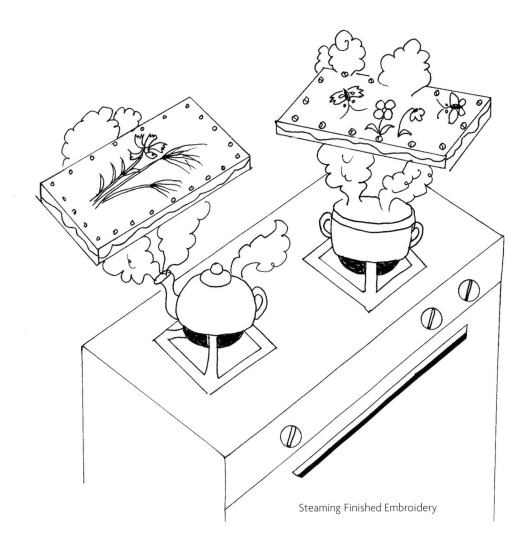

Steaming Finished Embroidery

DISASSEMBLING THE ARTWORK

Step 1 After the steaming is completed, let the embroidery dry for 1 or 2 hours.

Step 2 Remove the pushpins.

Step 3 If you will be storing the piece, back the embroidery with cardboard the same size as the fabric and secure it in place temporarily with masking tape around the edge.

Step 4 Prior to framing your work, you must remove the masking tape from the cardboard.

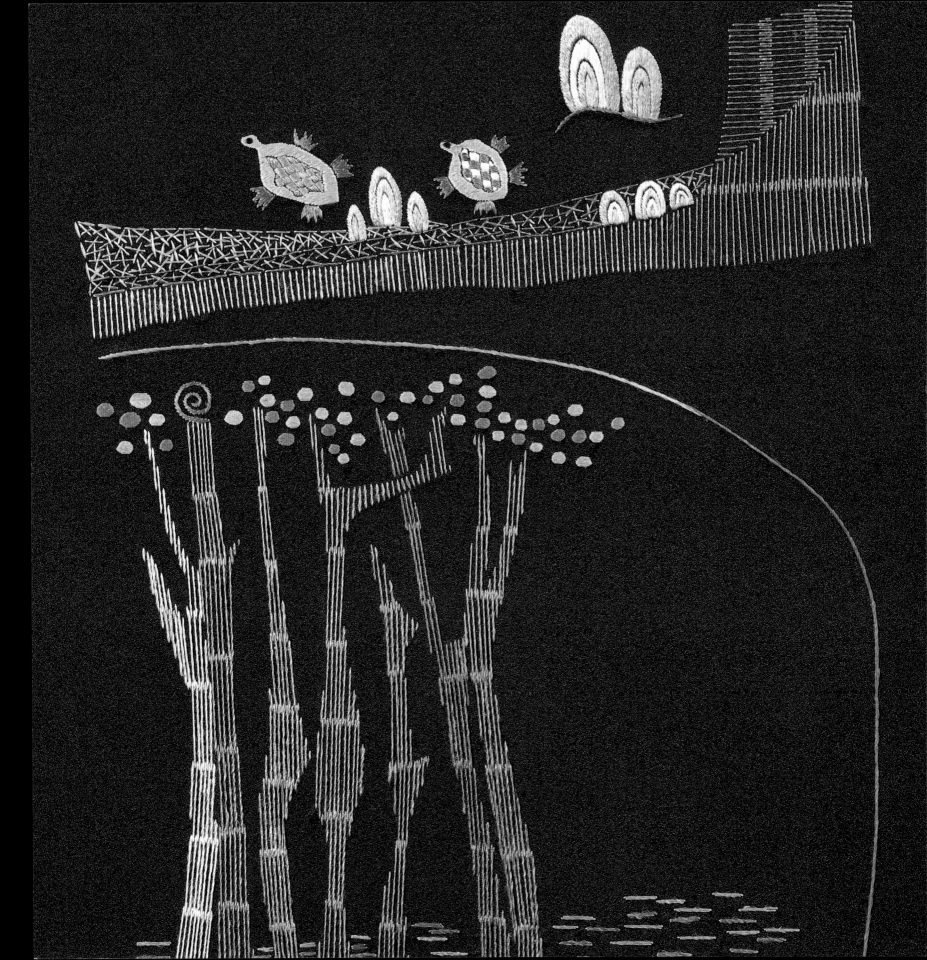

INSTRUCTIONS FOR PROJECTS

IMPORTANT NOTES AND TIPS BEFORE YOU BEGIN

Although the author provides specific colors to be used in each piece, feel free to be creative and choose your own colors. For convenience, a chart of the colors specific to each project is provided at the top of the first page of instructions for each of the 19 projects. The color tabs are labeled with either the number of the silk thread, or simply the name of the color, which refers to the metallic threads used in that project (except white and black). Details about the metallics, if any, are found in the instructions. All color tabs are close approximations of the actual color. You can also refer to the master works in the photographs to get an idea as to the colors that are used and how they are distributed throughout the piece. In general, no more than 1 or 2 skeins of each color are required for each of the projects, unless otherwise noted. The color chart that was referenced is the commercially available six-ply DMC sample embroidery floss chart. Sometimes the author refers to a color without giving a number—in these cases, you don't need a specific color number and can use any brand or type.

For each project the author gives recommendations as to what types or brands of thread are best to use. The brands include: Soie de Paris, Soie Perlee, Splendor, Kreinik (for metallic threads only), Silk Mori, Empress, Au ver a Soie, and DMC silk floss. The author also uses silk thread from Korea (see List of Suppliers on page 173). Commercially-twisted thread is recommended for these projects, but all types of twisted thread can be used. The working thread can be any length, but the length that is generally recommended is 18 inches.

If you need to purchase needles, the author recommends buying a packet of quilting needles. The size she prefers is 5, but feel free to make your own selection. Choose a needle with as large an eye as you can find for easier threading.

All dimensions given for each project are in inches and reflect the entire finished piece, not just the design area. Height is given first, followed by width in inches. Some of the diagrams are smaller than the given dimensions check dimensions and enlarge to desired size.

To determine the amount of fabric and the size of frame, or stretcher, needed for a project, take the dimensions provided and add three inches on all sides. This gives you the extra fabric you need to glue and tack it on to a frame.

Fabric color is suggested for many of the projects, but where not given you can match the color as shown in the photograph, or choose your own background color.

For all projects, please refer to the overview chapter beginning on page 46 for explanations and illustrations of the stitchery techniques.

Previous pages, left:
Turtles in the Ocean, Project 7, page 121

Previous pages, right top:
Bicycle Pouch, Project 15, page 157

Previous pages, right bottom:
Spoon Cases (Korean, Choson dynasty, 19th century). In the early 19th century spoon cases like these were embroidered by the bride-to-be for her dowry. These cases are stitched with numerous longevity symbols including cranes, pine trees, turtles, bamboo, sun, and water waves. The thunderline border represents long life, and the red background symbolizes happiness and marriage.

Opposite:
The author's signature at left is rendered in satin stitch. The top two Chinese characters mean *xiwu,* or "embroidery." The next two characters represent the Korean meaning of Young Yang Chung, which is "snow" (third character) "garden" (fourth character). The red character at the bottom is the author's name in Korean. Together it means "Embroidered by Snow Garden, Young Yang Chung."

Right:
Homecoming, detail of a four-panel screen showing pine needles and textured bark on the trunk.

For each project, the patterns in the far background should be completed BEFORE those in the foreground, especially when creating pine needles. Not only does this help create a more attractive piece, since previous mistakes can be covered up with the foreground stitchery, but it also helps to impart a more realistic perspectival effect.

In the diagrams, the small arrows are indicators of stitchery direction.

The traditional East Asian method of rendering a signature is in bright red. If you choose to sign your work, any stitch can be used, but the outline stitch is most highly recommended for a small signature. Look at other signatures to get ideas, such as the author's seen at left on page 98 and page 100 (last name Chung is in a circle). Another example on page 122 shows a signature in which the negative area is stitched in white and the red ground fabric shows through in the shape of the signature. Other examples appear on pages 129, 149, and 166.

Remember, for supplies consult the List of Suppliers on page 173 or your local embroidery or art supply shop.

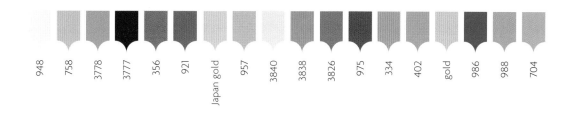

PROJECT 1: FLYING CRANE

(page 100)
Dimensions: 9 x 9 inches
Embroidered by the author

The flying crane and pine tree design seen on this highly stylized vessel, which was created by the author for an embroidery class, is rendered in five different versions of the satin stitch: diagonal, straight, horizontal, leaf, and fanning. The satin stitch is the most basic of all embroidery techniques, and once mastered, even a complicated-looking piece such as the *Flying Crane* can be completed by a beginner, with concentrated effort, within a few days.

The feathers on both of the wings of the crane are rendered in diagonal satin stitches of varying lengths, the short and long stitches alternating along the outer contours to achieve a feathery visual effect. The tail feathers utilize a leaflike stitch as seen in diagrams B and F on page 103. The pine needles are created with straight satin stitches laid out in a fanlike arrangement like real pine boughs. The clouds on either side are also executed with straight satin stitches, but these are sewn in the horizontal (weft) direction, while the red thunderline pattern in the background is created using the fly-stitch method (diagram E). To achieve a curved, sculptural effect for the tree trunk, cotton-sheet padding is placed underneath the finishing stitchery (pages 50 and 104).

NOTE: In transferring the design for *Flying Crane* there is no need to draw every detail of the thunderline pattern that appears behind the crane. If it's easier, you can apply dots to indicate the lines.

MATERIALS

Fabric: 65% silk/35% nylon plain weave in dark blue
Thread: Soie de Paris or Splendor; Kreinik gold and silver or white rayon metallic.

STITCHERY

Step 1 Start with the "leaves" in the lid on the top of the vase and work from right to left, completing leaf 1, 2, etc. in numerical sequence (diagram A, page 103). Begin stitchery of each leaf on the right side of the center "vein," making stitches that extend from the top right to the left in the diagonal direction using light peach #948, and work downward in the leaf-stitch technique (diagram B), leaving a 1-millimeter space in the center of each leaf for the vein. The right side of leaf 2 is stitched in the same technique with the right half of the leaf stitched with light peach #948 and the left half with peach #758. Finish the veins in outline stitch (page 60) in #948 for leaf 1 and magenta #3778 for leaf 2.

Step 2 Leaves 3 and 4 are stitched with peach #758. The veins are completed in #3778 in the outline stitch.

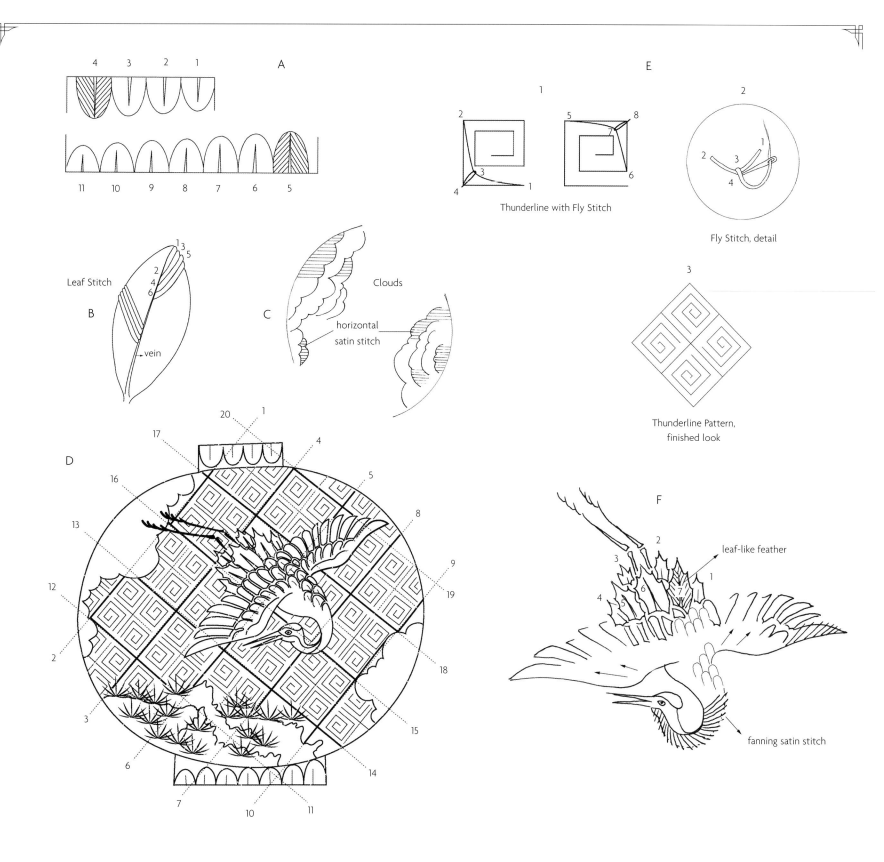

A

E

1

Thunderline with Fly Stitch

2

Fly Stitch, detail

Leaf Stitch

B

vein

C

Clouds

horizontal
satin stitch

3

Thunderline Pattern,
finished look

D

F

leaf-like feather

fanning satin stitch

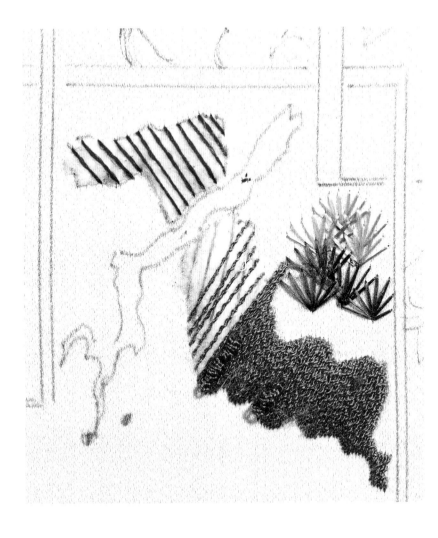

Step 3 Leaves 5 and 6, on the base of the vase, are completed in light peach #948. Use #758 for the veins.

Step 4 For the right half of leaf 7, use #948, and for the left half use #758. Use #3778 for the veins.

Step 5 Leaves 8 and 9 are stitched with #3778. Use #3777 for the veins.

Step 6 Leaves 10 and 11 are embroidered with medium magenta #356. Use #3777 for the veins.

Step 7 The cloud in the upper left is completed in horizontal satin stitch, with the outer edges stitched in darker colors and the inner areas in lighter shades. Start at the areas of the cloud labeled 1, 2, and 6, using magenta red #3777 (diagram page 102).

Step 8 For the area of the cloud labeled 4, use light magenta #921.

Step 9 For the areas labeled 5 and 7, stitch with a single strand of Japan gold #7 or 8; you will have to separate these strands, and use only a single one for the stitchery of these areas.

Step 10 For area 3, use magenta red #3777.

Step 11 The cloud on the lower right is also completed in horizontal satin stitch. For area 8 use Empress white thread; for area 9 use light pink #957; area 10 use blue #3840, and for area 11 use darker blue #3838.

Step 12 Now start on the tree trunk. First, lay a cotton sheet on the trunk area and secure it with straight stitches over the cotton, laid diagonally from left to right with a 4-millimeter space between each stitch (photo this page, and page 50).

Step 13 Start the finishing stitchery for the trunk. These satin stitches are stitched right to left diagonally, in the opposite direction as the securing stitches holding the cotton in place, using brown #3826 for the half of the trunk toward the left and darker brown #975 on the right of the trunk (page 100).

Step 14 To create the bumpy texture of the pine bark, use the bullion-knot stitch (page 81). You may use textured thread like chenille or wool yarn to achieve a rougher, more textured effect (see this page and page 99 for examples of bumpy-textured bark).

Step 15 Start creating the boxes for the background design, the thunderline pattern, using medium magenta #356 for the area to the top left of the crane and a darker shade #3777 for the area to the crane's right. The guideline stitches are created by laying long satin stitches diagonally across the entire vase. These stitches are spaced approximately 28 millimeters apart and make a diamond-shaped grid. The needle comes up at 1 and goes down at 2, crossing the vase diagonally (diagram D). Next, the needle comes up at 3, goes down at 4, and so on until 10, as indicated in diagram. All of these long threads are laid across the surface of the fabric and couched down at intervals of 4–5 millimeters apart with thread of the same color. You must stop the long stitches at the contours of the clouds, crane, and tree motifs, taking the thread down beneath the fabric, and then coming back up on the other side to continue with the guideline.

Step 16 The second set of guidelines is created similarly, but with darker magenta #3777 and crossing in the opposite direction of the first set. The needle comes up at 11, goes down at 12, and so on until the grid is completed at 20. Again, these threads must be secured by couching.

Step 17 Within each diamond-shaped box that you have created with the guidelines, create four smaller boxes by bisecting the larger box on each of its four sides (diagram E-3). Use thread that is the same color as the outermost box.

Step 18 Start making the thunderline pattern by making fly stitches (diagrams E-1, 2). Using this technique, the needle comes up at #1 and goes down at #2; the loose thread is pulled gently to corner #3 and then couched down at #4.

Step 19 Repeat these steps for the other corner. The needle comes up at #5, goes down at #6, the loose thread is pulled gently to corner #7 and couched down at #8 (diagram E-1). Repeat this process until all the diamond-shaped boxes are filled with a square thunderline design, making sure that the starting point remains open, like a square spiral.

Step 20 Now start on the crane. The wings and feathers are embroidered in satin stitch, leaving space in between the

feathers to expose the background and delineate the individual feathers.

Step 21 The scalelike feathers on the back of the crane are stitched with thin silver and gold threads, using satin stitch. You may substitute white rayon metallic thread. You must start the feathers from the bottom, at the base of the tail, and work up toward the neck (page 102).

Step 22 For the neck, use straight stitches that are gently fanned out at the outer contour (diagram F).

Step 23 The leaflike tail feathers in the back are completed in the leaf-stitch technique (diagram B). For tail feathers 1, 2, 3, and 4 use dark blue #334, and use peach #402 for the larger tail feathers 5, 6, and 7 (diagram F). Leave a 1-millimeter space for the vein in the center of each.

Step 24 The veins of the tails are created in outline stitch (page 60) with gold metallic thread of about 0.5-millimeter thickness.

Step 25 Now start the wings. First, use the outline stitch to delineate the shoulders from the neck to the tip of the longest feather on the end of each wing. The long feather on the end of the right wing is embroidered using satin stitches of alternating lengths that extend outside the contour to achieve a feathery effect (diagram F). Repeat for the long feathers on the left wing. This technique is the same as that used for fish fins (see Project 18).

Step 26 The beak and foot are created in outline stitch (page 60, technique B) using gold thread with a thickness of about 0.5 millimeter.

Step 27 The crown is completed in seed stitch (page 56) with bright red thread.

Step 28 Lastly, the pine needles are stitched using dark green #986 for those in the back, medium green #988 for those in the middle ground, and lighter green #704 for those in the foreground (diagram below). Feel free to stitch pine needles over the trunk and over previously made pine needles, as this creates a more naturalistic effect (page 100).

Pine-Needle Stitch

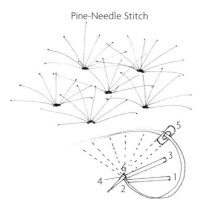

Step 29 The vase is delineated with gold couching (page 66) along the outside edge, using Japan gold #8 thread with a thickness of about 0.7 millimeter. The contours of the vase are outlined with four strands of couched thread (two sets of two threads couched together, side by side), while the base of the vase is delineated with six strands of gold thread (three sets of two threads side by side). Use red threads to couch down the gold threads.

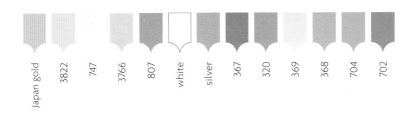

Japan gold | 3822 | 747 | 3766 | 807 | white | silver | 367 | 320 | 369 | 368 | 704 | 702

PROJECT 2: MORNING GLORIES
(page 107)
Dimensions: 12 x 9 inches
Embroidered by Kim Kum-Ja, Korea

The flat, thin petals and bright hues of these summer flowers make them inviting subjects for the embroiderer's art. The inspiration for this project comes from the sight of sunlight falling on the morning glories growing by the author's kitchen window.

The application of subdued color on the large petals of these beautiful blossoms is reminiscent of Asian ink painting. This project is also an exercise in the blending of colors using needle and thread, with the shades of light blue at the outer contours gradually darkening toward the center of the flower, which in turn provides a lovely contrast for the white stamens.

MATERIALS
Fabric: 65% silk/35% nylon blend
Thread: Au ver a Soie or Empress (flowers); Splendor or Silk Mori, Kreinik silver metallic (polyester), gold and white metallics

STITCHERY

Step 1 The bamboo must be stitched first, before the flowers. The bamboo sticks are created with Japan gold #7 or 8 laid vertically, which are couched down (page 66) with yellow #3822 thread.

Step 2 Stitch all the joints (diagram A, page 109) of the bamboo in diagonal satin stitch with a single strand of Japan gold #7 or 8 (separate out the individual strands that make up the one thread; you want only one of these strands, otherwise it will be too thick for the fabric). The joint area can be padded with thread padding if you wish (page 50).

Step 3 The flower petals are divided into three sections—top (or outer area), middle, and bottom (or inner area)—each of which is embroidered in a different shade of blue (page 108 and diagram B). The petals are then highlighted with silver thread over the finishing stitchery. Start by delineating the contours of each of the petals with outline stitch (page 60, technique A) before beginning the long and short stitches (page 53), which will fill the petals with subtle gradations of color.

Step 4 When the outlines are finished, start the long and short stitches to fill in the petals. The needle comes up at the

368

320

368

747

3766

807

white metallic

3766
747

807

747

320

367

367

367

320

320

369

vein
368

369

320

704

702

367

807

747

3766

367

contour along the outer edge of the petal, and goes down one-third of the way into the petal. Use light blue #747 for the first row, making sure to leave the area for the stamens (this page, C) free as you work your way into the petal (this page, B).

Step 5 For the middle area, use medium blue #3766 in long and short stitches. Don't forget: the short stitches meet the long stitches already stitched in the outer area, and the long stitches meet the short ones.

Step 6 Repeat this stitchery for the innermost and third area, using dark blue #807.

Step 7 Finish the stamen (or vein) in straight satin stitch with white metallic #5272 embroidery floss (diagram C). Repeat Steps 4–7 for all the petals.

Step 8 The bud on the bottom right (p. 108 and diagram D) is embroidered in diagonal satin stitch with light blue #747 for the outer (top) contour and medium blue #3766 for the middle and bottom portions. For the petal in the center, use dark blue #807.

Step 9 You can highlight all the petals with satin stitches of silver metallic thread, scattered wherever you'd like the light to catch the stitchery.

Step 10 The trumpet-shaped bottoms of the blossoms, should be stitched in long and short stitches using dark blue #807 for the top portion (directly underneath the opened petals) and light blue #747 for

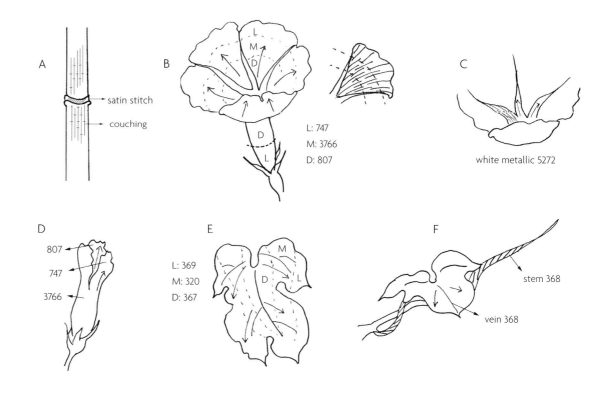

A — satin stitch — couching

B — L: 747 M: 3766 D: 807

C — white metallic 5272

D — 807 747 3766

E — L: 369 M: 320 D: 367

F — stem 368 — vein 368

the bottom portion (nearest the green leafy bud case).

Step 11 Since the areas to be stitched for the leaves are rather large, the veins in the center should serve as dividers of the leaf into sections and as a starting point for each stitch in those sections. As indicated by the arrows in diagram E (this page), the needle comes up at the center vein at the top and goes down and outward in long and short stitches toward the contour using dark green #367 for the inner area closest to the veins, medium green #320 for the middle section, and for the outer contour of the leaf use light green #369. The lengths of the stitches should measure approximately 1 centimeter for the short stitches and 1½

centimeters for the longer stitches. Use light green #369 on the underside of the top leaf.

Step 12 The veins on the leaves are embroidered in outline stitch using green #368.

Step 13 The areas of the bud cases (or shells) are stitched with satin stitch in green #704 for the tips and #702 for the bases.

Step 14 For the winding stems (this page, F), use the thickest form of outline stitch (page 60, technique C). Start at the bottom of the picture in dark green #367, and as you work upward change to medium green #320, and end at the top and ends of stems with a light green #368.

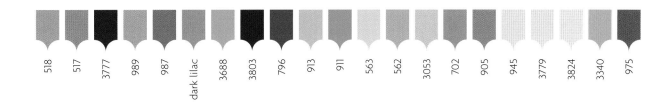

| 518 | 517 | 3777 | 989 | 987 | dark lilac | 3688 | 3803 | 796 | 913 | 911 | 563 | 562 | 3053 | 702 | 905 | 945 | 3779 | 3824 | 3340 | 975 |

PROJECTS 3 AND 4: MINI-GARDEN— CHRYSANTHEMUM AND GREEN RADISH LEAF

These two small designs were adapted from an antique Qing dynasty embroidery and modified for beginners. The *Chrysanthemum* diagram for transferance varies slightly from the photograph. It is recommended that you follow the diagram but feel free to copy the piece in the photograph.

CHRYSANTHEMUM

(page 110)
Dimensions: 5 x 5 inches

MATERIALS

Fabric: Silk satin weave in light beige or off-white
Thread: Splendor or Empress, Kreinik

STITCHERY

Step 1 Start with the curved tips of the blue flower petals using light blue #518 and stitch with diagonal satin stitches (page 46). The lower, narrower portions of the petals will be stitched in darker blue #517. To blend the light and dark blues, stitch about a third of the way down the petal in light blue, leaving several unstitched spaces approximately the width of the thread to be filled in with the dark blue later (flower petal detail, page 112).

Step 2 Fill in the blank spaces between the last few light blue stitches with dark blue #517, and then finish the remainder of the petals with the same dark blue, all in diagonal satin stitch.

Step 3 The darkest petals, shown in black (page 112, diagram A), are highlighted in a very dark red #3777 using the satin stitch. There are more darkened petals in the master work in the photograph than in the diagram—you can choose the number of petals you'd like to darken.

Step 4 The small leaf on the top right (page 112, A) is stitched with light green #989 and the small leaf beneath the flower, on the right, is stitched with darker green #987.

Step 5 The big leaf on the left of the stem is rendered in two shades: the top half is stitched in light green #989 and the bottom with #987, using conventional leaf-stitch technique (page 103).

Step 6 The veins of the leaves, the dots on the butterfly wings, and the antennae on the large butterfly are stitched with dark lilac nylon metallic thread.

Step 7 The butterflies are optional—the author added them to the diagram to improve the composition. For the large butterfly, the larger wings are stitched

Flower Petal

517

518

Blending with two shades

darkened petals

leaf 1

with light magenta #3688 and the two small wings are rendered in darker magenta #3803, all in satin stitch. The antennae are rendered in outline stitch (page 60) with dark lilac nylon metallic thread. The body and eyes are stitched with dark blue #796, the body in satin stitch and the eyes in seed stitch.

Step 8 For the small butterfly, the larger wings are embroidered in green #913 and the bottom wings in #911, all in satin stitch. The dots on the larger wings are stitched in dark lilac nylon metallic thread. The antennae of the small butterfly are rendered in outline stitch with light magenta #3688. For the body and eyes, do the same as for the large butterfly.

GREEN RADISH LEAF

(page 113)

Dimensions: 5 x 5 inches

MATERIALS

Fabric: Silk satin weave, mustard yellow

Thread: Splendor or Empress

STITCHERY

Step 1 Leaf 1 is embroidered in two shades of green, the top portion in light jade green #563 and the bottom with darker jade green #562 in the leaf stitch technique (page 103). Leave a space for the wide veins in the center of each leaf.

Step 2 Leaf 2 is embroidered with silver green #3053 for the left side and #702 for the right side. Leave the holes in the leaf free from stitchery (diagram B, above, and page 113).

Step 3 Leaf 3 is embroidered all in green #905 or you can use colors as shown on page 113.

Step 4 Leaf 4 is embroidered using the same colors as Leaf 2 (light on top, dark on bottom), or all in silver green #3053.

Step 5 The wide central veins of the four leaves are stitched using beige #945 in the outline stitch that goes slightly over the finished green stitchery of each leaf.

Step 6 Shorter vein stitches start at the edge of the large veins and fan outward across the leaf, forming a decorative pattern. The short veins of Leaf 1 are embroidered with salmon pink #3779; for Leaf 2, white; for Leaf 3, #3779; and for Leaf 4, #3779. Use a long stitch for each branch of the vein (page 113).

Step 7 The dainty flowers are stitched in satin stitch with two shades of pink: #3824 for the petals of flowers A and B, and #3340 for the remaining flowers. Use as much of each pink as you'd like.

Step 8 The stems of the flowers are embroidered in outline stitch with dark brown #975. This color is also used for the tiny dots at the center of the flowers (diagram B).

Step 9 Create a frame with gold thread couching (4 strands as in the contour of the vase in Project 1), or you can finish with Rainbow Gallery Ribbon (secure along the edges of the ribbon with stitches). You can find the ribbon at Nordic Needle (see List of Suppliers, page 173).

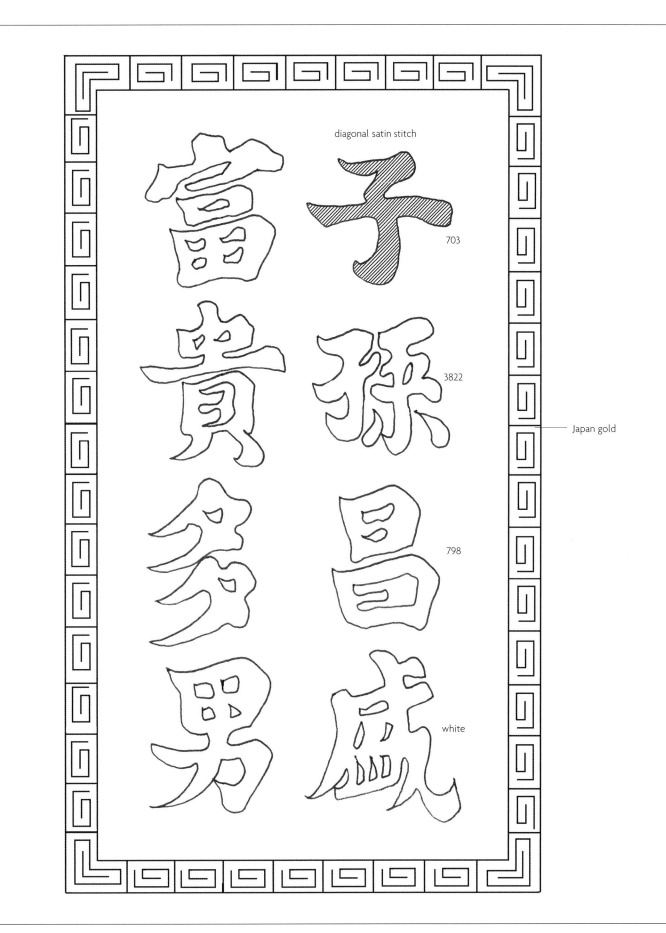

diagonal satin stitch

703

3822

Japan gold

798

white

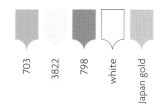

703 · 3822 · 798 · white · Japan gold

PROJECT 5: GOOD WISHES FOR THE BRIDE *(page 114)*
Dimensions: 7 x 3 inches

This design is adapted from an antique Korean spoon-and-chopstick case (page 114) and modified to be suitable as a bridal gift. The author took the key design that forms the border around the nature scenes on the front of the antique cases appearing on page 97, bottom, and combined it with auspicious Chinese characters in Korean verse to create the case in this project. In Korea, this type of object traditionally would be made by the mother of the bride.

The characters are read starting with the figure at top right, down the column, then back up to the top character in the left column, and down again. They are pronounced in Korean *boo gui da nam, ja son chang sung* and can be translated as "wealth, honor, many male offspring" on the left, and "descendants will be prosperous" on the right. The words convey good wishes for a newly married couple's future. The colors of the piece also extend favorable wishes, as they represent the five directional colors of East Asian cosmology and signify a balance of the yin and yang.

MATERIALS
Fabric: Silk satin, red
Thread: All types of threads can be used, such as Soie de Paris or DMC six-strand embroidery floss; border: gold paper–wrapped thread (also known as Japan gold) or twisted silk thread or synthetic metallic thread.

STITCHERY
Step 1 Start stitching at the top right character, working downward in diagonal satin stitch (page 115). The first row (top two figures) are green #703, the second row is yellow #3822, the third row is blue #798, and the bottom row is white.

Step 2 When the characters are completed, the thunderline surrounding the characters is created with gold couching. Use the conventional couching technique (page 66) with Japan gold #7 or 8, and couch the threads down with the thinnest machine-made red thread. For the outer line (border) of the key design, two strands of Japan gold or yellow #3822 are couched side by side with red thread. Repeat for the inner line.

Step 3 For the thunderline patterns use the fly-stitch technique (page 103), or you can use the straight stitch, each stitch 1–1½ centimeters long and secured down with the same red thread every ½ centimeter or so. This is probably the most straightforward method.

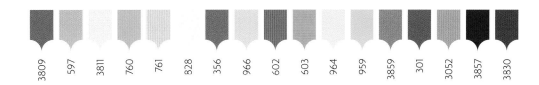

3809 597 3811 760 761 828 356 966 602 503 964 959 3859 301 3052 3857 3830

PROJECTS 6 AND 7: THE FOUR SEASONS—PINK BIRDS IN THE SKY AND TURTLES IN THE OCEAN

(two of four panels are presented here)
Embroidered by students at the former
International Embroidery School, Korea

The scenic patterns shown in these highly stylized, fantastical Asian-style landscapes were popular with textile designers and embroiderers in the 1970s. In Asia, natural forms such as clouds, rocks, and water were often depicted together with deer, turtles, and birds to create a pattern that symbolized longevity. Such compositions were particularly popular on home accessories. Virtuous brides often presented their new parents-in-law with gifts ornamented with longevity symbols as a gesture of filial piety. The turtle motif, symbolizing longevity, was also popular among Japanese embroiderers, rendered on traditional wedding robes (*uchkake*) and presentation cloths (*fukusa*, page 37), to express wishes for the bride's long life and happiness on her wedding day.

PINK BIRDS IN THE SKY
(page 118)
Dimensions: 13 x 10 inches

MATERIALS
Fabric: 65% silk/35% nylon-blend satin
Thread: Soie de Paris or DMC six-ply embroidery floss

STITCHERY

Step 1 The blue sky in section A (page 119) at the top (background) is embroidered in the star-cross stitch technique (page 65). Start on the right and work to the left using blue #3809 for the top right, #597 for the middle section, and #3811 for the left.

Step 2 Stitch the flowers in section A in satin stitch in any combination of pinks #760 and #761 and blue #828.

Step 3 The trunks of the flowering trees are created in long, vertical, loosely interlocking mat stitches (page 63) of no more than two rows. Use brown #356.

Step 4 The green ground behind the trunks is done in long horizontal straight stitches in green #966.

Step 5 The birds in section B are stitched with long satin stitches. The body of the bird in the foreground is stitched in pink #602, the top wing in pink #603, and the bottom wing in blue #828. For the body of the bird in the background use #828, use blue #964 for the top wing, and blue #959 for the bottom wing.

Step 6 For the trees in the middle section C, first make guidelines using straight stitches, stitched horizontally, about 1–2 centimeters apart.

Step 7 The trees are then stitched in vertical mat stitches (page 63), about 1–2 centimeters in length, over the previously made horizontal guidelines, leaving a 1-millimeter space in between each mat stitch in the first row to allow for the interlocking stitches in the second row. For the second row, the needle comes up between the stitches of the first row, about 2 millimeters in to interlock the two rows, and then goes down about 2 millimeters past the next guideline. Repeat this process for all of the trees. The colors used are (from the far left tree trunk to the right): #3859, #3811, #356, #301, #966.

Step 8 Horizontal stitches are made in #3052 behind tree trunks in section C.

Step 9 In section D the tree stumps are rendered in vertical straight stitch with the following colors (from far left trunk): #3857, #301, #301, #966. The slightly curved horizontal lines directly above the trunks are stitched in #3859 (at right) and #3830 (at left).

Step 10 For section E, first make a vertical guidelines with green #966, then embroider horizontal mat stitches in the same color.

Step 11 Repeat the star-cross stitch in section F in colors #3859 and #3830 where specified on page 119.

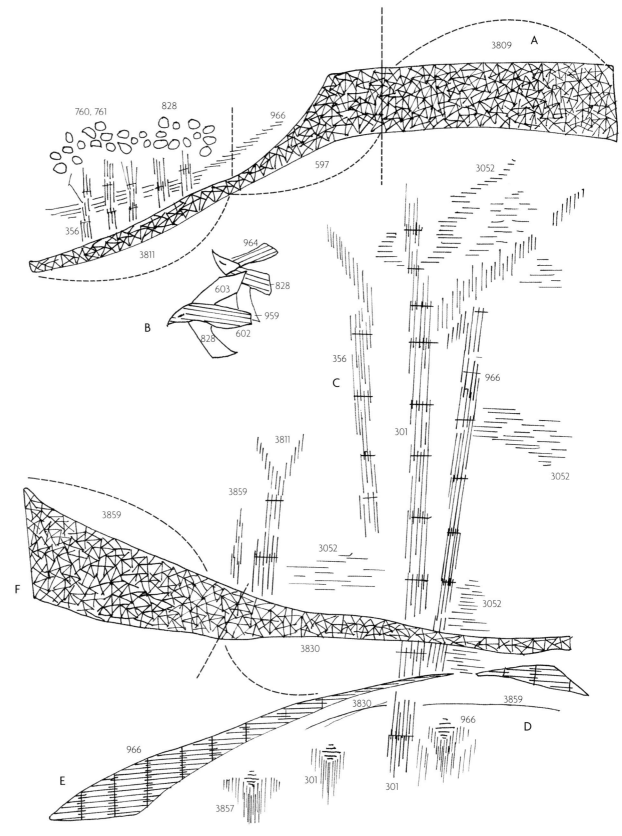

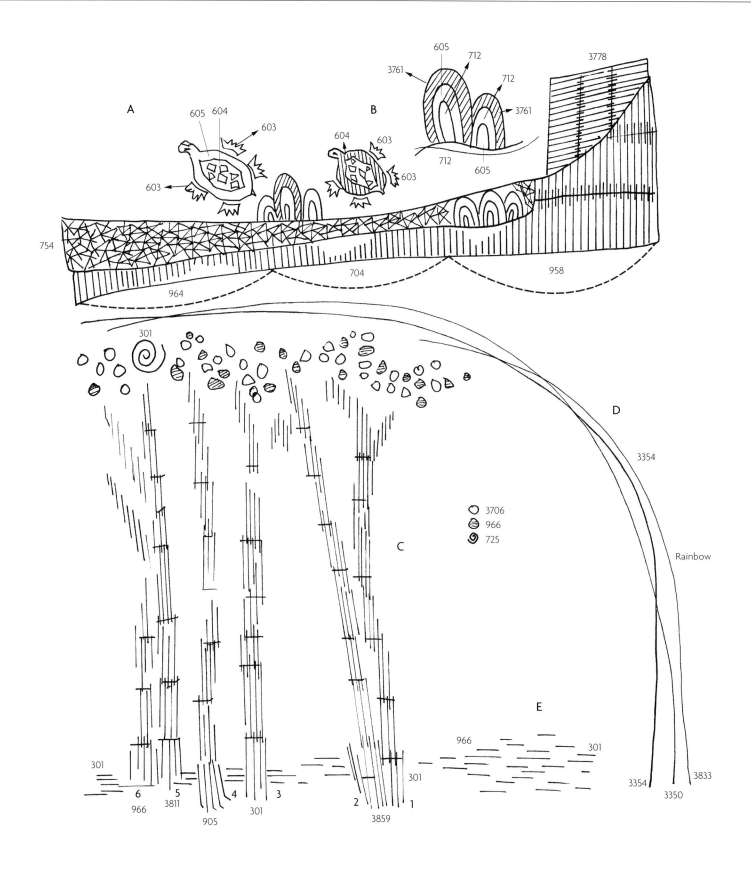

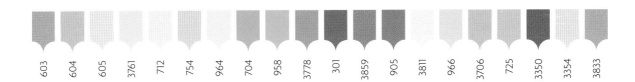

TURTLES IN THE OCEAN

(page 96)

Dimensions: 13 x 10 inches

MATERIALS

See page 117

STITCHERY

Step 1 All elements in the turtles and the abstract water waves (rainbowlike shapes) in sections A and B at the top (page 120) are embroidered in diagonal satin stitch. Start stitching at the contours of the turtles and the three groups of water waves. The turtles are embroidered in three tones of pink—#603 (feet), #604 (shell), #605 (head and body)—and light blue #3761 (spots on the shell). The checkerboard shell on the turtle at right is stitched in blue #3761 and white. The water waves are done in colors pink #605, beige #712, and blue #3761, in varying combinations of your choice or follow master work on page 96.

Step 2 The sand-colored water below the turtles is embroidered in the star-cross stitch (page 65) in pinkish-beige #754. (Two colors are shown on page 96, but the author has simplified this piece for the beginner. You decide how you'd like to render this section.)

Step 3 The blue area beneath the water is embroidered in the vertical mat stitch (page 63) with horizontal guidelines in shades of green and blue: #964, #704, #958. The brown area to the right and above the blue is also rendered in the mat stitch with pinkish-brown #3778.

Step 4 All the trees in section C are embroidered in mat stitch. First make the horizontal guidelines, then make the vertical satin stitches over top of these, leaving a 1-millimeter space between the stitches to allow for the interlocking of rows. Each tree is rendered in a different color: tree 1 is done in #301, tree 2 #3859, tree 3 #301, tree 4 #905, tree 5 #3811, and tree 6 #966. (**NOTE:** These colors differ slightly from the master work.)

Step 5 Each of the small flowers floating above the trees in section C is embroidered in satin stitch with four different colors: #3706, #966, #725, and #301. You may choose how to distribute the colors. The spiral is completed in the outline stitch (page 60) using #301.

Step 6 The three lines arching over the trees in a rainbow (section D) are embroidered in outline stitch in #3350, #3354, and #3833.

Step 7 The ground foliage in section E is embroidered in a simple satin stitch with green #966 and brown #301.

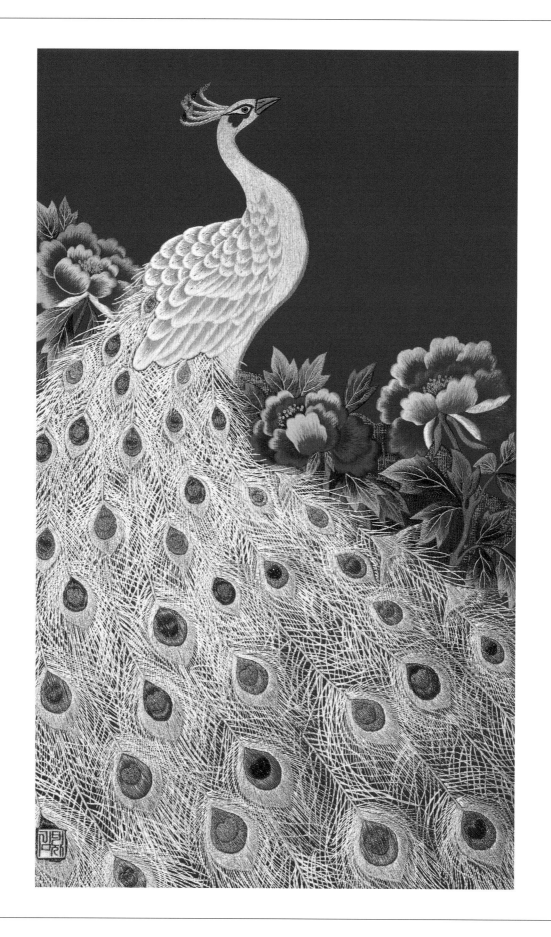

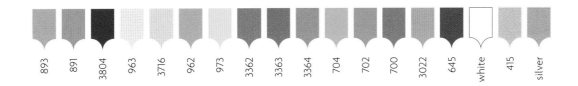

PROJECT 8: WHITE PEACOCK WITH PEONIES *(page 122)*

Dimensions: 22 x 14 inches
Embroidered by Kim Tae-Ja, Korea

Peacocks and peonies are traditional symbols of wealth in East Asia. Depicted together, they represent wishes for prosperity. Cascading peacock tails can be rendered in a number of ways with readily available threads and fabrics. For the white peacock against a red background shown here, the tail is elaborately rendered, with the individual feathers overlapping in a complex, naturalistic web.

The embroiderer who created this piece used hand-twisted silk of 20 filaments twisted into each thread (thickness of 0.9 mm) for the scalelike feathers on the back and the splinters (long, wispy feathers that come off the main feather vein) of the tail feathers. The main veins of the tails were rendered using a combination of rayon with silver twisted into a thread with a thickness of 1½ centimeters, using non-devisable DMC metallic thread.

MATERIALS

Fabric: 65% silk/35% nylon
Thread: For the flowers—Splendor, Au ver a Soie or Empress; for the scales and body of the peacock—Soie de Paris or Soie Perlee; for the splinters of the tail feathers—silk floss; for the main vein of the tail feathers—DMC rayon silver metallic; for the eyes of the tails, the crest, and the peacock's eye—Kreinik nylon metallic (various colors, your choice—refer to pages 122 and 126)

NOTE: Each petal on the flowers requires approximately three yards of thread.

STITCHERY

Step 1 First stitch the flowers, starting with flower A. All contours of all the petals are first prepared in outline stitch (page 60). Next, place a cotton sheet on the inner portion from the contour of petal #1 of flower A, spread evenly, and secure it with stitches in the diagonal direction (use same color as finishing stitchery), leaving 2 millimeters of space around the contours (page 50).

Step 2 Begin stitching over the padding in the opposite direction of the securing stitches starting at the contour of petal #1 in the long-and-short-stitch technique (page 53), working your way inward, using light pink #893 for the first row.

Step 3 For the second row, the stitchery must proceed outward, starting at the middle area. Use pink #891.

Step 4 For the third row, use pink #3804, again stitching outward.

Step 5 The two far petals (8 and 9) are rendered with pink #893 for the first row (top) and #891 for the last row (bottom).

Step 6 The petals in front (10 and 11) are embroidered last with lighter shades of pink: #963 for the first row (top), medium pink #3716 for the second row, and #962 for the inner portion (bottom).

Step 7 The seeds in the center of the flowers are stitched in yellow #973, using the extended seed stitch (page 56).

Step 8 Repeat the above steps for flowers B and C.

Step 9 Next, start the leaves, all of which are rendered in the leaf stitch (page 103). For the leaves on flower A, the needle comes up at the center vein, and the stitchery proceeds diagonally outward toward the contours in dark green #3362, medium green #3363, and light green #3364. To determine how much of each color to use, refer to page 122. Start with dark in the center and use lighter tones as you work toward the contours to give the leaves a realistic appearance.

Step 10 The veins are embroidered in outline stitch with green #704.

Step 11 The remaining leaves are rendered in the leaf-stitch technique with greens #704, #702, and #700.

Step 12 The rocks peeking from behind the flowers are embroidered in well stitch (page 65), using ready-twisted textured thread (such as wool yarn or chenille) in gray #3022 and brown #645. A different texture can be achieved with a two-strand thread: hold one strand taut while pulling the other strand down along the taut strand; the second strand forms loops around the first. Couch down desired length of "textured" thread. This method resembles the bullion-knot stitch (page 81).

NOTE: As you stitch the peacock, the scales and feathers should be stitched starting at the tail and moving upward toward the neck, since they overlap from top to bottom. This is especially true for the elaborate tail of the peacock: start stitching the very long tail feathers at the bottom of the tail and work up toward the body, overlapping the feathers as you go to create a naturalistic, weblike appearance. The images on pages 126 and 127 demonstrate this effect to perfection.

Step 13 The contours of all the scalelike feathers on the back of the peacock are first completed in outline stitch (page 60). These feathers are then stitched over thread padding (pages 50 and 52).

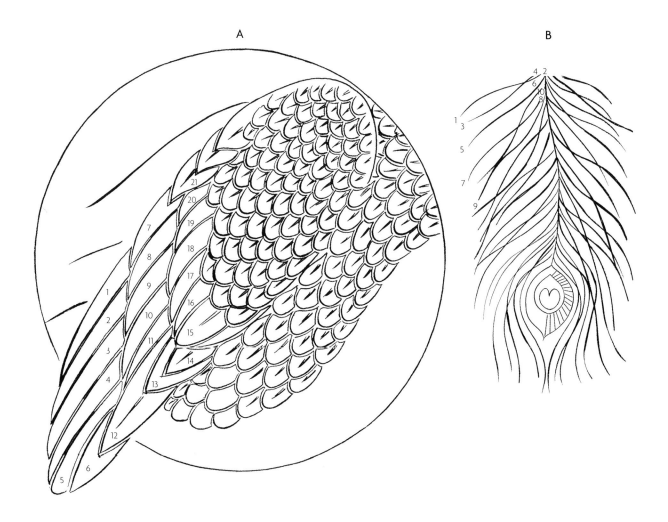

A

B

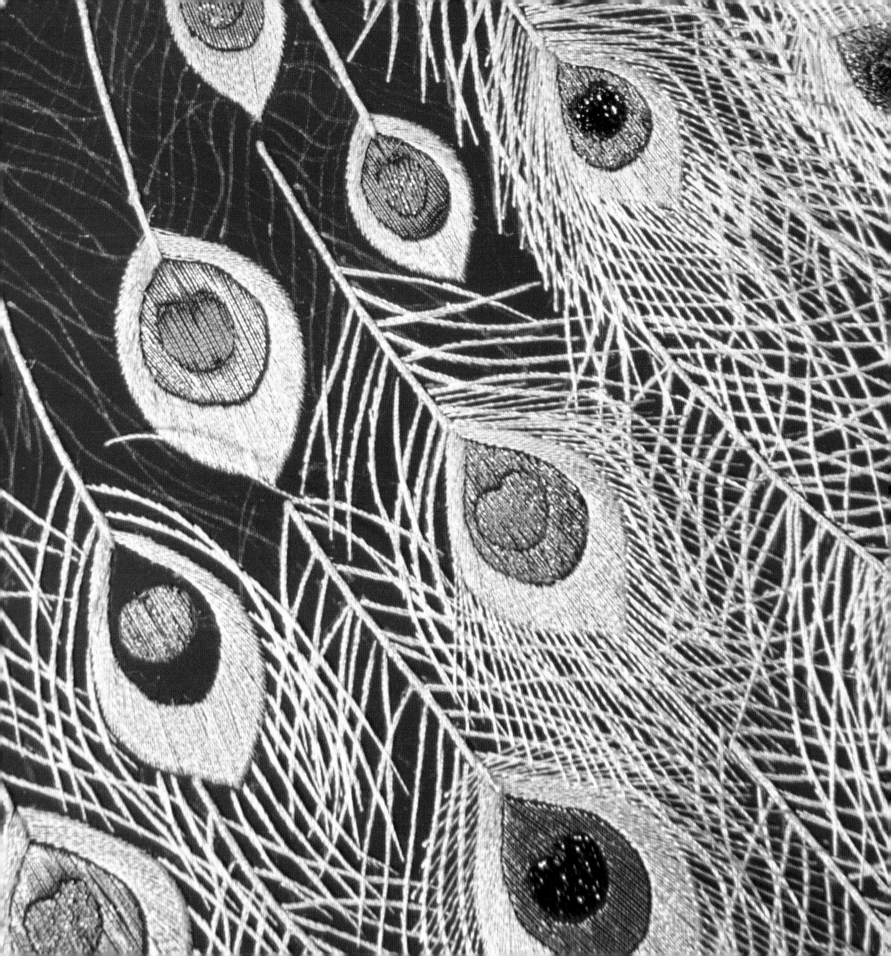

Step 14 Start at feather 1 (page 124, diagram A), and work inward in straight long and short stitches with white thread. Leave the inner area free for the blending-in of gray (page 122). Complete feathers 2–21 in the same method.

Step 15 The smaller feathers on the back are stitched in white in satin stitch.

Step 16 Blend the inner areas of all the feathers with gray #415 in long and short stitch on the larger feathers and satin stitch on the smaller feathers.

Step 17 Repeat the same stitchery for the small scales near the neck. The stitches in the ending scales are gradually merged into the body area with irregular satin stitches.

Step 18 The center veins of the smaller feathers are highlighted with silver metallic thread in outline stitch. For the long veins of the longer feathers, make one single straight stitch extending from the top of the feather down the center almost to the bottom with silver metallic thread. Then secure down with white thread spaced 1–1½ millimeters apart (page 124, A).

Step 19 For the body, stitch in irregular satin stitch in the vertical direction going up toward the head with white threads that are thinner than those used for the feathers (approximately 0.7 millimeter thick).

Step 20 For the peacock's comb surrounding the eye, make seed stitches in red (page 56).

Step 21 The five small crests on the head are stitched with rayon metallic threads in satin stitch of various bright colors at the tips. The long stemlike part is stitched in silver metallic. Colors used in the crest as well as the eyes of the luxurious tail include various shades of pink, green, blue, teal, purple, gold, and silver metallic (pages 122 and 126).

Step 22 Start to create the long, wispy feathers surrounding the eyes of the tail feathers and coming off the long veins. Use long satin stitches of 2–3 centimeters in length. These stitches can be left loose or secure, depending on your preference. The image at left shows a loose style, the image at right a more packed style.

Step 23 The contours of the outer part of the eyes of the tail feathers (page 124, B) are prepared in outline stitch with white thread, prior to the final stitchery.

Step 24 Stitch the outermost eyes of the tail feathers in vertical satin stitch with a single strand of white metallic thread, leaving 1 millimeter of space between each of the eyes.

Step 25 For the second and centermost eyes of each of the tail feathers, repeat the same steps as for the outermost eye (except the outline stitch on the contours) using any variety of vivid hues in metallic thread. (Refer to pages 122 and 126.)

Above:
White Peacock with Peonies, detail of an 8-panel screen embroidered by the author in the 1960s. This was the first time she used polyester metallic thread, a new product at the time.

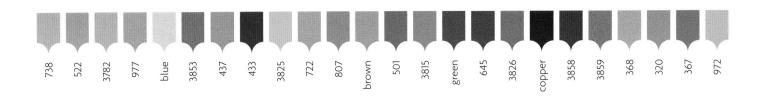

738 522 3782 977 blue 3853 437 433 3825 722 807 brown 501 3815 green 645 3826 copper 3858 3859 368 320 367 972

PROJECT 9: BIRDS WITH GRASSHOPPER ON ORCHID

(page 129)
Dimensions: 11 x 6 inches
Embroidered by Deborah Bowers, USA
(Embroiderers' Guild of America member)

MATERIAL

Fabric: 100% silk damask pattern, with clouds and Daoist symbols (if desired)
Thread: Kreinik metallic and Empress or Splendor

STITCHERY

Step 1 Start with the bird on the right, which is rendered in irregular-length satin stitches in beige #738, on the belly and head (page 131, A). The accent colors are embroidered in random long and short satin stitches (page 53) with deep gray #522 and grayish-beige #3782. Make sure these stitches are well blended. Accent with brownish-orange #977 on the chest and neck area, and above the beak, using alternating satin stitches on top of the previous stitches.

Step 2 Next, complete the bird on the left using the same colors: beige #738 in irregular satin stitch, then #522 and #3782 to highlight in the same stitch (page 131, C). Then highlight the area under the neck with touches of #977.

Step 3 Each bird's eye is filled in with satin stitch, using white thread, and the pupil is stitched with metallic blue thread in a solid blue dot. The beaks are completed in diagonal satin stitch with orange #3853. Add touches of red to accent the beaks, and the feet are embroidered in outline stitch (page 60) in #977.

Step 4 For the bird on the right, the tail feathers are embroidered in a leaf stitch (pages 103 and 131, A and B) with beige #437 and accented with darker beige #433. Every two or three stitches insert a darker beige stitch. The stitches meet at the center of each tail feather, but leave the center free of stitches, allowing ground fabric to act as the vein. The tails at the end are further highlighted with orange #3825 in alternate stitches, mostly on the tips, using the thinnest threads. (Refer to page 129 for distribution of colors.)

Step 5 The grasshopper is embroidered next, using diagonal satin stitch in orange #722 for the body, neck, and head, and blue #807 for the wings. The dainty legs and antennae are created in black with the long stitch. The legs are couched at the joints with the same color as the wings, blue #807. The antennae are couched with a vibrant brown shimmering metallic thread. The feet are stitched in the same blue as the joints.

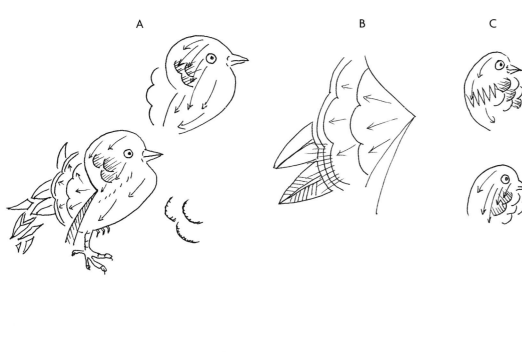

A B C D

E

Step 6 The rock formation along the left edge is stitched with moss green #501 on the lower portion, lighter green #3815 for the top area, and highlighted with metallic green in well stitch (page 65).

Step 7 The reddish-brown rock (this page, D) is stitched in the well stitch using a combination of gray #645 and red-brown #3826, and highlighted with copper metallic thread over top. The bottom-most portion of the rock is rendered in well stitch, with darker brown #3858 and #3859 in the middle.

Step 8 The peony leaves are completed in leaf stitch with green #368 for the left half of the leaf, and green #320 for the right. For the veins and stems use outline stitch in green #367.

Step 9 The long, thin orchid leaves in the center (this page, E) are rendered in diag-

onal satin stitch with green #368 for the tips blended in with green #320 for color gradations. The curved area that catches the light is usually done in lighter shades.

Step 10 The orchids are embroidered with diagonal satin stitch in white, and the seeds are rendered with seed stitch in yellow #972.

Step 11 The peony petals are stitched in the long and short stitch, inserting antique orange #722 on the inner portions and light orange #3825 on the outer portions.

Step 12 The braided thread used for the edging, as seen on page 129, in which the embroiderer applied braiding technique using hidden stitches, is optional. Another simpler option is to couch down double strands of gold metallic thread side by side, couched down with the thinnest machine-made thread in red.

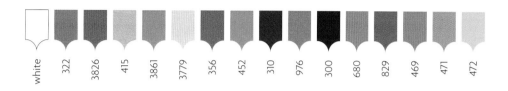

white | 322 | 3826 | 415 | 3861 | 3779 | 356 | 452 | 310 | 976 | 300 | 680 | 829 | 469 | 471 | 472

PROJECT 10: CELEBRATION

(page 132)
Dimensions: 26 x 18 inches
Embroidered by Lee Byung-Sook, Korea

A majestic white crane perched on a pine tree represents one of the most popular themes in East Asian painting. The crane, regarded as king of all flying creatures, is ranked among the most frequently used East Asian embroidery designs throughout the dynastic period and remains widespread as a longevity symbol. On New Year's Day, crane patterns are commonly displayed as symbols of happiness and long life.

Crane patterns are also found on embroidered items given as birthday gifts to elders, as well as on insignia badges made for court officials. From the introduction of insignia badges during the Ming dynasty, cranes symbolized first-rank civil officials, the highest level of the influential Confucian literati class, in China, Korea, and Vietnam. The carefully embroidered double-crane insignia (pages 34 and 35) emphasized the wearer's high rank at court and thus his elevated social status during Korea's Choson dynasty.

MATERIALS

Fabric: 65% silk/35% rayon-blend blue satin
Thread: Silk Soie Perlee or Soie de Paris. Rayon, six-ply embroidery floss, and cotton can also be used.

NOTE: Approximately 35 yards of white thread is needed to complete each crane. About two yards of that will be required for the largest areas of each of the wings (shoulder, or top of the wing, plus the two longest pointed feathers at the wing tips).

STITCHERY

Step 1 Start with the outermost, longest feather on a wing of crane A and work inward. Prepare the contours of all the feathers in outline stitch (page 60, technique B). Then, stitch over the contours with diagonal satin stitch.

Step 2 After completing the feathers on both wings, start with the scalelike feathers on the back of crane A. The satin stitchery must proceed upward from the tail area toward the neck area, leaving a 2-millimeter space between the scales (with the ground fabric visible) for insertion of outline stitches. Finish by inserting outline stitches between the scales to cover any uneven satin stitches.

Step 3 For the shoulders (tops of the wings), use satin stitches that extend inward in the diagonal direction as directed by arrows in the diagram on page 135 (inset A). Leave a 1-millimeter space at the top of the wings, then insert for the outline stitches.

Step 4 Start the rear tail feathers (four to six per bird) in leaf stitch, using gray-blue #322, leaving the center vein free of stitches. After completing all the tail feathers, finish the veins in outline stitch with reddish-brown #3826.

Step 5 For the long necks, start from the head area and work diagonally downward toward the belly, using diagonal satin stitch with white thread. For the dark area of the neck, use gray thread #415 in diagonal stitch (see page 135, inset A, and page 1).

Step 6 The bird's bill is created with diagonal satin stitch, using beige #3861 and pink #3779 for the tongue (if there is one).

Step 7 For the crown, use antique red #356, stitched in seed stitch (inset A and page 1).

Step 8 The birds' legs and feet are couched with two strands side by side of gray #452, with a thickness of about 1 millimeter. Couch with the same thread.

Step 9 The eyes are stitched first with black #310 in seed stitch, and the white around the black is done in satin stitch with white thread.

Step 10 Start the trunk of the tree, using vertical straight stitches in red-brown #976 for the main section of the trunk and darker brown #300 for the bark; scatter the trunk with couching stitches in a variety of browns to achieve an aged appearance. Texture can also be expressed with the bullion-knot stitch (page 81) placed at various points on the surface of the trunk.

L: 471
M: 472
D: 469

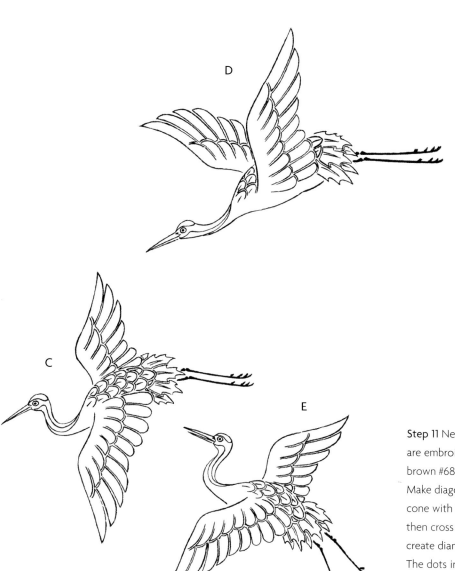

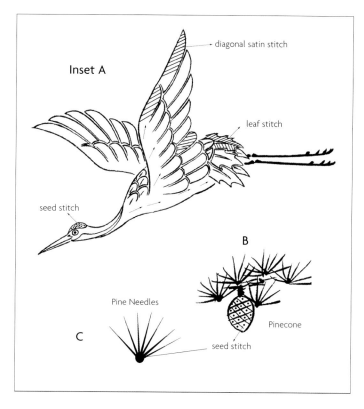

Step 11 Next, start the pinecones, which are embroidered in satin stitch in light brown #680 prior to the pine needles. Make diagonal trailers across the pine-cone with long stitches in one direction, then cross in the other direction, to create diamond-shaped boxes (inset B). The dots in each box are made in seed stitch with dark brown #829.

NOTE ON THE PINE NEEDLES: The instructions given in Step 12 are for a method different from that which appears in the photo on page 132. The artist who embroidered that work rendered the pine needles in the traditional Korean stitchery technique, embroidering the darkest needles in the foreground, the lightest in the background, and all the needles stitched over thread padding.

Step 12 The pine needles are stitched in the fanning method (page 105 and inset C). For each bunch (or fan) of needles start the stitchery on the far right side, using a satin stitch of about 1½–2 cen-timeters in length, and proceed to the last pine needle on the left. For color, start with dark green #469 for the pine needles in the far distance (at the top of the tree), medium green #471 for the mid-dle ground, and light green #472 for the needles in the foreground (at the bottom of the tree). For distribution of the differ-ent shades in the pine needles, refer to the diagram on page 134. At merging point of each set of needles, finish with one to three seed stitches in dark brown #300. The overlapping of pine needle stitches over each other and the trunk of the tree is desirable for creating the most natural-istic, three-dimensional effect.

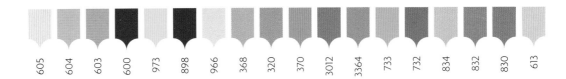

PROJECT 11: PAMPAS GRASS AND COSMOS *(page 137)*

Dimensions: 15 x 10 inches
Embroidered by Ha Young-Soon, International Embroidery School, Korea

The seasonal cosmos and pampas grass both bloom during the autumn months. The small pink petals and velvety yellow stamens of the cosmos provide a particularly pleasing subject to capture with needle and thread.

MATERIALS

Fabric: 65% silk/35% rayon-blend satin
Thread: Empress or Splendor

NOTE: One yard of thread is needed for each flower petal.

STITCHERY

Step 1 Starting at the outer edges of the petals, stitch in the straight satin technique using light pink #605 (on the outer area), medium #604, and dark #603 (inner area). The outer edges of the petals should be notched in appearance (page 138, A and B).

Step 2 Embroider the innermost section of the petals with the darker pink #600 in long and short stitch in dramatically different lengths (page 137).

Step 3 Embroider the center of the flowers with yellow #973 in the horizontal satin stitch and then decorate with vertical extended seed stitch (page 56) in darker brown #898. The stamens are rendered in a scattering of extended seed stitches.

Step 4 The bud (page 138, C) is embroidered in two shades of pink: #604 for the outer edges and #603 for the inner area in satin stitch.

Step 5 The leaves of the flowers (page 138, D) are each embroidered with diagonal satin stitch. Use light green #966 on the pointed ends, #368 for the middle areas, and #320 for the inner areas.

Step 6 The ends of the long, thin, pampas grass leaves are finished in beige #370 for the ends and greenish-brown #3012 for the remainder of the leaf, all rendered in straight stitches of irregular lengths.

Step 7 Stitch the stems of the pampas grass (page 138, E) and flowers next, from top to bottom, using beige #3364 for the top, #733 for the middle, and #732 for the bottom.

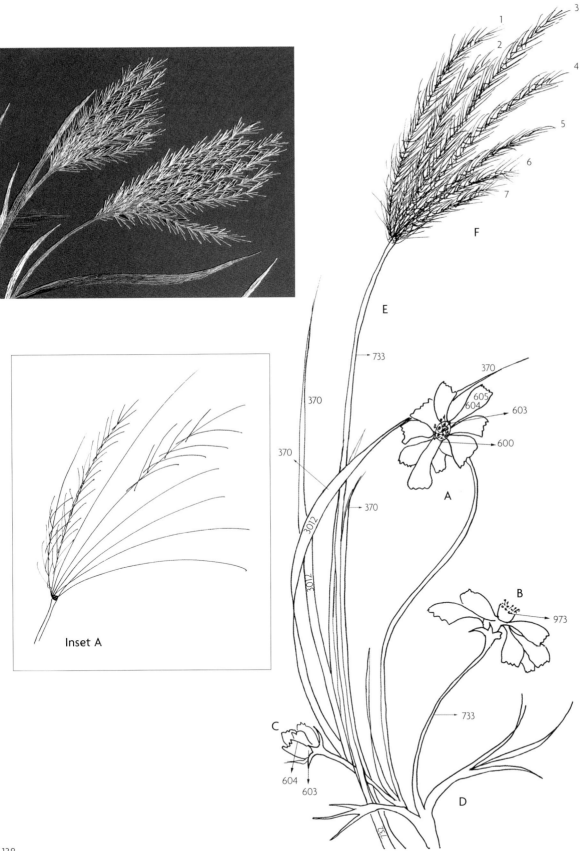

Inset A

Step 8 The seven lines of the main veins of each length of hirsute grass (this page: F, inset A, and photo) must be completed in outline stitch first to form the guideline, using light brown #834.

Step 9 The hirsute grass at the top is rendered in the splinter stitch: each of the single hairs is one straight stitch, and they all overlap one another (see photo and inset, this page). The grass is stitched in three colors: #832, #834, #830.

Step 10 Start by making a single splinter (or hair) of about 1½ centimeters in satin stitch with #832 to the left of the vein, then repeat on the right side. Repeat the stitchery, leaving a 2-millimeter space in between each stitch so that the next stitch can be inserted.

Step 11 For the second step, squeeze satin stitches of about 1 to 1½ centimeters in length between the previously made stitches in #832.

Step 12 For the third step, stitch over the previous stitches using brown #830. In other words, lay splinters over these stitches using darker thread to create a three dimensional effect. Highlight with light beige #613.

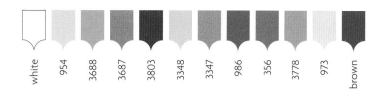

white 954 3688 3687 3803 3348 3347 986 356 3778 973 brown

PROJECT 12: MAGNOLIA I

(pages 140–141)

Dimensions: 20 x 40 inches

Embroidered by the author

Magnolia blossoms, with their long, lobed petals, are reminiscent of the lotus flower, and in fact, the Chinese word for magnolia literally translates as "tree-lotus," pronounced *mok-ryun* in Korean. Traditional symbols of prosperity, spring-time, and purity, lotus flowers were pop-ular motifs for dowry items and a favored pattern for Korean wedding robes.

This composition of six blossoms and six buds on a branch is embroidered in long and short stitch with three shades, and all are stitched over the cotton sheet underpadding (also known as stump work). The author embroidered this piece with loosely hand-twisted thread in a thickness of about ⅓ millimeter. Project 12 was created by the author as an exper-iment with padding techniques. Various padding techniques can be observed in a number of historical examples, such as the Daoist priest's robe (page 15, bottom), *fukusa* (page 37, turtle), and the Japanese wedding robe (pages 2–3, turtles).

MATERIALS

Fabric: 65% silk/35% polyester-blend in navy blue

Thread: Empress or Splendor; silk floss or six-ply cotton embroidery thread can also be used; Kreinik rayon metallic

STITCHERY

Step 1 Start by making an outline stitch (page 60) along the contours of each petal on all the flowers.

Step 2 For cotton padding on the petals, place a cotton sheet in the middle of a petal and spread it out in both directions. The thickest padding, about 3–5 millime-ters high, should be in the middle, but the thickness should diminish in both directions to about 1 millimeter, leaving a space of about 2 millimeters along the inside from the contour of the flower free from padding (page 50). The middle petal, #5 on each flower (page 142, bot-tom A and B), should have the highest padded center.

Step 3 Secure the padded area by couch-ing down the cotton with thread in 4- to 5-millimeter intervals in the opposite direction of the finishing stitch (securing threads should be the same color as finishing stitches, white or pink). The padding for the buds should be thinner than that used for the petals of the open blossoms.

Step 4 Now fill in the petals. Flowers A, B, C, and D are embroidered in white. On flowers A, B, and C, petals 1, 2, 3, and 4 (page 142, top) should be embroidered first, leaving petal 5 for last. Petal 5 is stitched over petals 2 and 3. Flower C has 6 petals: stitch petal 5 second to last,

petal 6 last (page 142, bottom A). The final stitchery for the petals must proceed from the top (outer contour of petal) to the bottom (inner area near stamen), in the opposite direction of the padding stitches, using well-blended long and short stitches leaving one-third of a space for the next stitch measuring 1–1½ centimeters in length (page 53). For the first row of stitches on the petals, the needle comes up at the contour and goes down at the middle portion of the petal, working inward.

Step 5 For the second row of stitches insert short stitches to meet the long stitches of the previous row, working from the inside outward.

Step 6 For the third row of stitches, at the bottom (inner) area of the petals, insert short stitches in light green #954 to meet the long stitches of the previous row. This will give all the petals a very subtle greenish cast. Repeat for all the petals of the white flowers and buds.

Step 7 Flowers E, F, G, and H are stitched in light magenta #3688 on the outer area of the petal, medium magenta #3687 in the middle area, and dark magenta #3803 on the innermost area. Where the petal is curled up and the underside is showing (petal 4 on flowers E, F), use #3688.

Step 8 The magenta buds are stitched in the same manner as the flower petals, using two shades of dark magenta. For

the pointed area of the contour, use the lighter shade #3688, and for the inner area of the bud use the darker #3687.

Step 9 All the small leaves are embroidered in diagonal satin stitch in light green #3348 and darker green #3347, leaving the central vein free. Stitch the veins in outline stitch in green #986.

Step 10 The trunk should be stitched in irregular satin stitch following the lines of the trunk and branches. Use brown #356 for the trunk and a light brown #3778 for the young branches.

Step 11 The stamens are created with vertical satin stitch in yellow #973. The stamen seeds are completed in extended seed stitch (page 56) over the previously laid satin stitches, covering the surface, in brown #14 rayon metallic thread. (**NOTE:** this method will produce a look slightly different from that which appears on pages 140–141.)

Step 12 The three-pointed shells (or the bud cases at the base of the flowers and buds) are stitched in vertical satin stitch with brown #14 rayon metallic thread. To give the shells a more natural, fuzzy-looking texture, stitch short, spikey, straight stitches extending slightly beyond the contours of the shell, scattered all along the contours. Use a thinner thread for the spikes, if desired, for a more subtle textural effect.

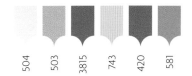

PROJECT 13: MAGNOLIA II

(page 145)

Dimensions: 16 x 8 inches

Embroidered by P .C., Hong Kong

There are many variations of the counted stitch (page 77), also known as canvas work. The counted stitch used for this project is similar to the brick stitch, in which weft (horizontal) and warp (vertical) threads are counted. Canvas work is done on mesh fabric, and it can either cover the entire background, or be combined with a variety of stitching techniques (page 81, fragrance pouch). This type of stitchery can also be seen in small items in Chinese embroidery, such as the tent stitch of the fan case (page 78) and the brick stitch of the pleated Chinese dragon skirt (page 77).

MATERIALS

Fabric: #22 mesh silk gauze in brown

Thread: Soie de Paris or rayon or cotton floss DMC or crewel embroidery. The thickness of the thread is important in this piece—the thread should be as thick as the holes of the mesh in the gauze; double the thread size by using two strands at a time, if necessary.

NOTE: When transferring this piece to the cloth, trace only the outlines of the flowers and buds. The "snowflake" pattern on the flowers and buds (page 145)

is created when wefts are left unstitched. The pattern is formed by a series of units, each unit consisting of three stitches, each stitch laid side by side, each crossing over nine wefts, the middle stitch starting one weft higher than the two side stitches. Two wefts are skipped after each of the three long stitches (see the shaded boxes on page 147), and another unit in the series is begun with the next set of three adjacent stitches crossing over nine wefts. Stitches will be shorter—crossing over fewer wefts—at the contours of the petals and buds. Follow the diagram of petal 3 on page 147 closely and apply the technique to all motifs. The master work on page 145 reveals a slightly different pattern on the branches and stems, which can be achieved by counting wefts in a slightly different formation than that described above.

STITCHERY

Step 1 You may begin by stitching petal 3 of flower C (pages 146 and 147). Start at the top of the petal with green #504. The colors of the magnolia flowers are blended with light green #503 in the middle of the petals, with the colors gradually darkening to a darker green #3815. (**NOTE:** This color pattern varies slightly from the master work on page 145—feel free to choose your own colors or follow the colors in the master work.)

(continued on page 147)

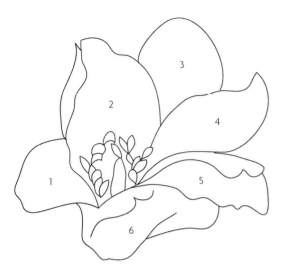

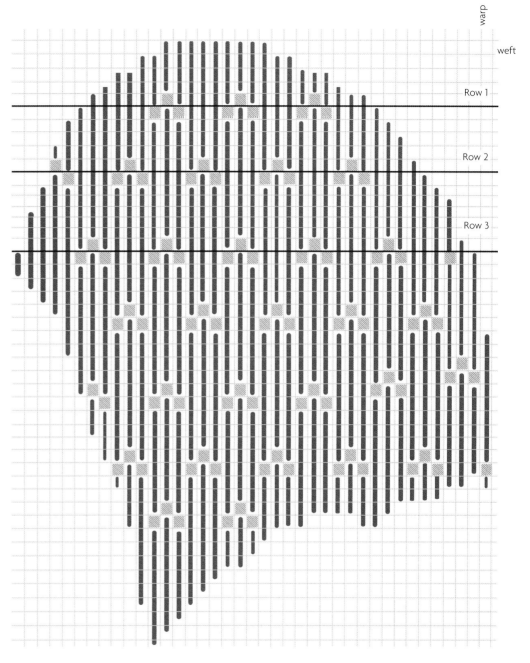

weft

Row 1

Row 2

Row 3

Petal 3 (detail) of Flower C

Step 2 Complete all petals in counted stitches (page 77), and over top of these stitches complete the centers of each flower in satin stitch with yellow #743.

Step 3 Use shorter counted stitches for the trunk, stems, buds, and bud shells. The brown for the trunk and bud shells is #420; the green for the stems is #581; the green for the buds is #503.

Step 4 For this piece, feel free to choose whatever counted stitch you prefer. The author recommends the brick stitch.

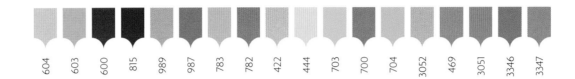

604 603 600 815 989 987 783 782 422 444 703 700 704 3052 469 3051 3346 3347

PROJECT 14: ROSE OF SHARON

(page 149)

Dimensions: 24 x 14 inches

Embroidered by Choi Jeong-In, Korea

The rose of Sharon, which blooms in a variety of eye-catching hues, is also known as the hibiscus. With their luxuriant, vividly colored flowers and abundant buds, blossoming rose of Sharon branches provide a particularly attractive subject for the embroiderer. This project, a hanging scroll depicting a rose of Sharon branch, is based on a ten-panel screen by the author entitled *Unified Korea*. The original screen (pages 154–155) was commissioned in the 1960s by the newly established South Korean government to serve as a symbol of national spirit, since the rose of Sharon, called *Moo-goong-hwa*, is South Korea's national flower. In creating this screen, the author sought to represent the vitality and perseverance of the Korean people through their 5000-year history with a design of hardy summer flowers on an aged tree trunk arranged in the shape of the Korean peninsula. The stitchery technique employed for this project, featuring long and short stitch in three shades of pinkish-purple for the flowers and three shades of green for the leaves, is relatively simple.

Master embroiderers of both the East and West have traditionally found inspiration in garden flowers. *The Roses* (page 151) is embroidered in conventional long and short stitch using threads in darker shades of red between the petals. The overlaying of rose petals represents one of the most complex skills required of the embroiderer. Keeping this in mind, the author designed large, fully opened flowers for this project.

MATERIALS

Fabric: 65% silk/35% polyester fabric in light eggshell

Thread: Soie de Paris or Soie Perlee or Splendor or Au ver a Soie (smooth).

NOTE: Artist Choi Jeong-In used approximately 8 yards of thread for each petal (includes padding and finishing stitches).

STITCHERY

Step 1 To begin, make short outline stitches along the contours of all flower petals.

Step 2 The flower petals are padded with thread padding on one-third of each petal to create a sculptural effect on the flat surface. Start the padding stitchery from the top (outer edge) to the bottom left (inner portion) of each petal, with horizontal stitches. Repeat the stitchery until one-third of the petal is covered, and then start to reduce the number of stitches by skipping stitches as you near the inner area, leaving about one-fifth of

the flower petal free (pages 50 and 52). Use the same color thread for both padding and finishing stitches.

Step 3 After the padding is finished, start to fill in the petals with long and short stitches (page 53), the long stitches measuring about 2 centimeters in length, and the short about 1½ centimeters. Start the first row of stitches from the outer edge of the petal (the needle must come up just outside of the previously made outline stitches and should proceed inward, covering the outline stitch). Use light pink #604 for the outer portion of the petals.

Step 4 For the second row, use medium pink #603, and start blending the colors by creating hidden stitches (page 53). These stitches must come up at the bottom of the second row, working outward, inserting short stitches to long stitches. Repeat in this manner for the third row (inner portion of the petal), using a dark pink #600, working outward.

Step 5 To finish the inner areas of the petals, dark raspberry #815 must come up at the innermost area of the petal on top of the previously laid stitches with thinner threads, using dramatically different lengths of long and short stitches, stitching outward (page 152, diagram 4, and page 153).

Step 6 The flower petals that are curled up, exposing the underside of the petal (page 152, diagrams 1 and 3), must be stitched last in diagonal satin stitches in #604.

Step 7 Delineate all the leaves with outline stitches, then fill them in with long

and short stitches. Starting from the outside edge of the leaf with light green #989, stitch the first row of long and short stitches, then the second row (inner area of the leaf) with green #987, leaving an open space of approximately 1-millimeter width between the two sides of the leaf for the vein (page 152, diagram 5).

Step 8 Next, complete the other side of the leaf in the same manner: #989 on the outer portion, #987 on the inner portion, leaving the vein free of stitches.

Step 9 Some of the leaves have brown tips (pages 149 and 153). Blend in with browns #783 or #782 on each leaf in long and short stitches inserted over top of the previously laid stitches.

Step 10 To make the vein, use the outline stitch (page 60, technique B), with light green #989. If you'd like to add more veins, stitch in outline stitch over top of the previously laid green stitches.

Step 11 The stamens are padded with thread in the diagonal satin stitch with beige #422, starting at the top left and working down to the right, repeating the stitch for the entire area of the long stamen, stitching in the opposite direction of the final stitchery. For a voluminous effect, use thicker thread for padding.

Step 12 The finishing satin stitch on the stamens must be stitched vertically from the tip of the stamen down to the bottom with beige #422, in the opposite direction of the padding, from right to left.

Above:
The Roses, detail.

Opposite:
Unified Korea, detail of a ten-panel screen.

Pages 154–155:
Unified Korea. This large ten-panel screen, embroidered by the author in the 1960s, was commissioned by the government of South Korea for the presidential mansion. The screen features a branch of the rose of Sharon, or hibiscus, designed in the shape of the Korean peninsula, the blossoms on the right representing North Korea, and those on the left representing the South. The composition symbolizes the hope for reunification as well as the tenacity of the Korean national spirit, since the hibiscus is known for its hardiness. Standing nine feet tall and fifteen feet long, this elaborate screen required more than three years to complete.

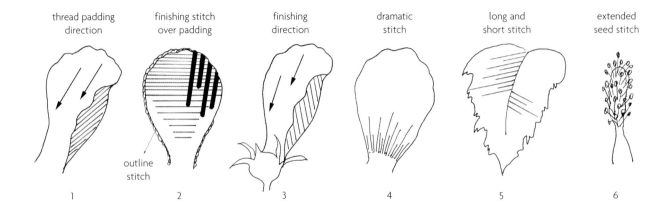

thread padding direction	finishing stitch over padding	finishing direction	dramatic stitch	long and short stitch	extended seed stitch
1	2	3	4	5	6

outline stitch

Step 13 Now create extended seed stitches of irregular lengths using yellow #444 (pages 56 and 150 and above, diagram 7). The stamen should be covered with these extended seed stitches.

Step 14 After the contours of the buds have been delineated with the outline stitch and the thread padding completed, begin filling in the buds. For the bud near the top on the right, begin long and short stitches that extend downward from the top right to the left in a slight diagonal. The half-opened petal at right is stitched prior to the center petal of the bud. The petal situated in front of the other petals should be the last one completed. Use the same colors as the opened flowers: #604, #603, #600.

Step 15 Lastly, the green bud cases visible underneath the buds must be stitched in #703, #700, and #704 (as indicated on page 153) with satin stitch.

NOTE: The stitches and thread color used to form tree bark can vividly express its age and texture. For example, the bumpy areas of the trunk seen on page 99 are created by embroidering satin stitches in the vertical direction, then highlighting with darker threads, and scattering bullion-knot stitches (page 81) across the surface. The rough and aged texture of the tree bark for the *Rose of Sharon* can be created using bullion knots or by adding loops made with textured threads, such as wool yarn or chenille.

Step 16 All branches (page 149) are embroidered in irregular satin stitch in the diagonal direction using various shades of gray from light gray #3052 to medium gray #469 to dark gray #3051. The trunk is created with evenly laid diagonal satin stitches using tightly twisted thread, and the bark on the very bottom of the trunk is highlighted with a darker shade of gray. The young branches toward the top of the tree are worked in the same manner of stitchery, with greens #3346 and #3347. (Refer to pages 149 and 152 for guidance as to where to apply each color.)

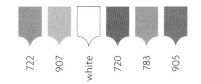

722 907 white 720 783 905

PROJECT 15: BICYCLE POUCH

(page 156)

Dimensions: 7 ½ x 6 ½ inches (entire pouch)

This project, which is based on the antique piece pictured at left (appliquéd by the author onto a pouch), can be used to decorate a pouch as shown or to embellish a picture frame or a pair of jeans or almost any cherished item. The peony is embroidered entirely in satin stitch. As the stitchery is quite simple and the piece is small, this design can be completed in a fairly short period of time. The pattern on page 158 has been slightly modified for this project. The author chose this project to demonstrate the ways you can adapt existing designs found on antiques or almost any artwork or decorative item to embroidery.

MATERIALS
Fabric: Plain-weave silk, black
Thread: silk embroidery floss

STITCHERY
Step 1 Start by filling in the five peach flower petals just outside of the small green petals. Use light peach #722.

Step 2 Next, stitch the five small green petals surrounding the center of the flower over the peach petals, using light green #907 in satin stitch. Make sure that the direction of the stitchery proceeds outward from the center of the flower.

Step 3 Now stitch the round stamen at the center of the peony, in horizontal satin stitch with light peach #722.

Step 4 The small leaves just outside of the petals that were stitched in Step 1 are completed in satin stitch with green #907.

Step 5 Start stitching the rest of the petals. Be sure to leave ground fabric free of stitches between these petals to emphasize their shapes. The first layer of petals comprise three areas of color: white for the innermost (bottom) area, dark peach #720 for the middle, and light peach #722 for the outer area (page 158, A). Start with the light peach #722 of each petal and work inward, finishing with white.

Step 6 Complete the stems using light brown #783 in outline stitch, working from left to right and downward.

Step 7 Now complete the leaves using the leaf-stitch technique (page 103), with the vein in outline stitch with brown #783. The right half of the leaves should be stitched with green #907 and the left half with green #905.

A

722
720
white

B

top: 905
bottom: 907

C

722
722 907

D

783

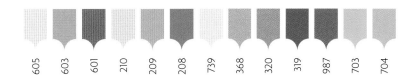

605 603 601 210 209 208 739 368 320 319 987 703 704

PROJECT 16: HYDRANGEAS

(page 160)
Dimensions: 9 x 13 inches
Embroidered at Jin Yuan Shan Textile
Studio, Harbin, China

The tiny, overlapping petals and large leaves of hydrangea branches are notoriously difficult to render two-dimensionally, even for skilled painters and embroiderers. This project demonstrates the versatility of the seed stitch, for the hydrangea flowers seen here have been rendered entirely in that stitch. Gradations of color are usually achieved through the use of the long and short stitch, but, as this project shows, a similar visual effect and a textured surface can be achieved through careful manipulation of the seed stitch.

NOTE: The master work on page 160 reveals a color scheme different from that which is suggested on page 161. The pattern on page 161 shows a color gradation of dark colors in the center toward light colors at the contours. This produces a more naturalistic effect, and the author recommends this method. Or, feel free to follow the master work.

MATERIALS
Fabric: pure white silk
Thread: Empress or Splendor or DMC silk floss

This self-instructional project is embroidered in simple, conventional seed stitch (page 56). Starting with the second row, the seed stitches must be made between the stitches of the previous row, so that there will be no gaps between the stitches. Refer to the diagram on page 161 for colors.

Flower A
L: 605
M: 603
D: 601

Flower B
L: 210
M: 209
D: 208

Flower Centers: 739

Leaves
L: 368
M: 320
D: 319
Veins: 368

Stems
1: 987
2: 703
3: 704

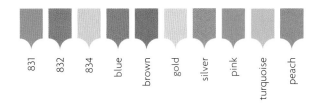

831 832 834 blue brown gold silver pink turquoise peach

PROJECT 17: BRONZE VESSELS

(page 163)
(two of eight panels are presented here)
Dimensions: each panel is 72 x 18 inches
Embroidered by the author

Bronze vessels, like those seen in the design of these two panels, are among the oldest surviving objects from East Asia's remote past. Originally used in ancient times in ceremonies of ancestor worship, exquisitely cast bronzes from the Shang and Zhou dynasties serve as potent reminders of the fundamental importance of filial piety and reverence for the past. As such, depictions of bronze vessels remain widespread as art motifs, and contemporary decorative arts continue to be fashioned in the shapes of these ancient forms. A 19th-century screen (page 28) illustrates a collection of such scholars' objects, depictions of which were favored for the decoration of scholars' rooms.

The author tried to capture on the two panels featured in this project not only the physical appearance of ancient bronzes, but also their symbolic importance in East Asian culture with the inclusion of a meaningful inscription. The four Chinese characters of the epitaph on the left panel, pronounced *chuan shi fu gui* in Chinese and *pak seo bu gui* in Korean, can be translated as "treasures

and honor to be handed down from generation to generation."

MATERIALS

Fabric: 65% silk/35% nylon blend
Thread: Soie de Paris or Soie Perlee;
Kreinik metallic; cotton or rayon (DMC)

STITCHERY

Step 1 Start with the panel on the left. For the top vase (page 164), start at the front right side of the rim and embroider in diagonal satin stitch with dark khaki #831 around one-third, leaving 1-millimeter space between stitches as you get close to one-third of the way around. Insert stitches of the next color, medium khaki #832, into these 1-millimeter spaces for smooth blending of the different shades. Repeat technique with light #834 for the center area. Repeat this blending technique in all of the motifs. Start again at the far left of the rim with #831, then #832, and then again #834—the center of the vase should be lighter to create a rounded, sculptural effect. Repeat for the base of the vase. All the accent trims of the vases are embroidered in diagonal satin stitch with khaki #834 for the light areas, #832 medium, and #831 for the darker areas, including the outside rim.

Step 2 Both handles are embroidered in diagonal satin stitch with #834 for the

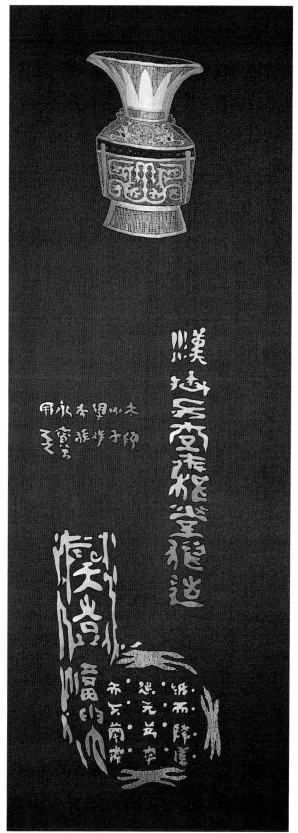

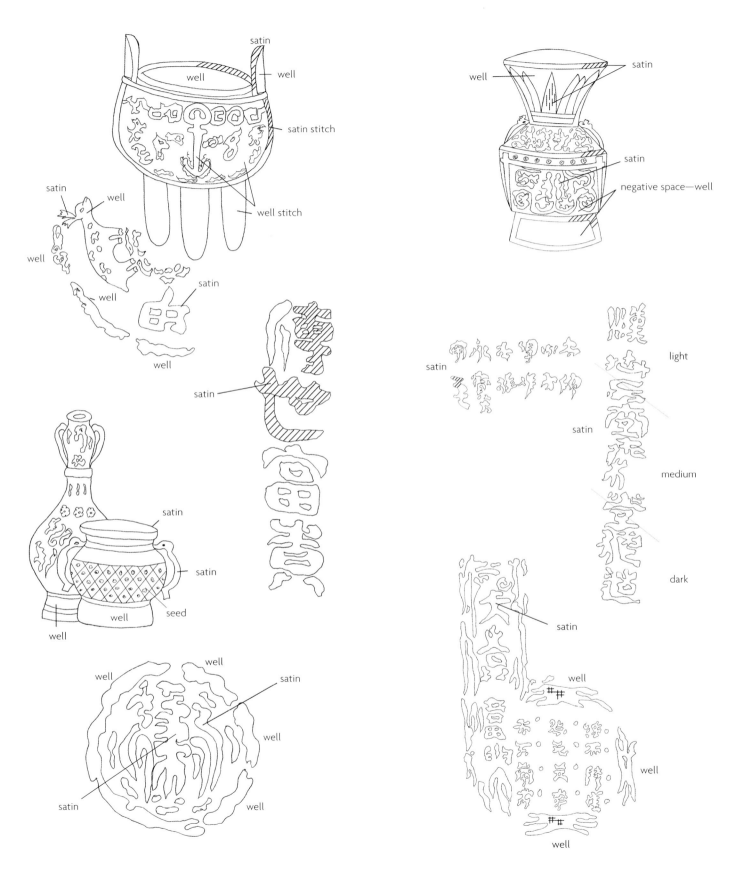

front, while the inner part of the vase and handles is embroidered in well stitch (page 65), the inner part of the vase with blue metallic thread, the inner part of the handle with brown metallic. Well stitches are embroidered on various areas of the whole piece with the three shades of khaki mentioned above. The front leg should be lighter than the two back legs.

Step 3 On the sides of the vase embroider the motifs in well stitch using blue, gold, silver, and brown metallic threads. For color distribution see page 163.

Step 4 The broken tiles in the foreground below the vase are embroidered in well stitch on the deer (except the antlers, which are in satin stitch). The characters to the right of the deer are in satin stitch. The pieces to the left and lower left of the deer are in well stitch, in the three shades of khaki, from the lightest starting at left to the darkest at right.

Step 5 The unbroken tile at the bottom of the panel is rendered using two techniques: the Chinese character is embroidered in satin stitch, starting at the top right and working downward to the left in the diagonal direction. From top to bottom, the coloration progresses from light to dark khaki. The borders around the character are embroidered with well stitches using the same coloration.

Step 6 The dainty bronze-colored vase in the middle of the panel behind the blue-green vessel is elaborately decorated by inserting pink and silver metallic threads in small patterns over top the previously

laid well stitches. All the areas except the small patterns are stitched in the khaki shades. The bronze and green vases are stitched in the same manner with rims and handles finished in satin stitch, the rest in well stitch. The green vessel utilizes the exposed ground fabric as a part of the design, and this is embellished by inserting gold dots created with shimmering threads. The trailers are in satin stitch with gold metallic thread in a cross-hatch pattern as shown (page 164). Insert a seed stitch (three wraps around needle) into the center of each diamond in gold metallic thread. Complete the rims of the vase in satin stitch with blue #3845, and fill in the rest of the space with well stitch using the same color.

Step 7 The four characters on the right are embroidered in slanting satin stitch using the three tones of khaki. Start with the lightest shade at the top and gradually darken as the embroidery extends downward.

Step 8 For the panel on the right, start with the vase at the top. Apply the diagonal satin stitch to all decorative, patterned (positive space) areas in the three shades of khaki (dark #831, medium #832, light #834). All background (negative space) areas are completed in the well stitch. Stitch the inside of the top of the vase in well stitch with blue metallic; the small handles on the sides are stitched in a turquoise metallic. The flowers across the front bar are created with satin stitch in brown metallic thread with the black ground fabric as background. The highly decorated area beneath the black bar is

embroidered as follows: a brownish-peach metallic thread is used on the background, and the motifs are finished in satin stitch with the three khaki shades.

Step 9 The rest of the decorative motifs on the second panel are embroidered in diagonal satin stitch in the three khaki shades, except for three areas at the bottom, which are completed in well stitch. Use the three shades to create a rounded, three-dimensional effect. (Refer to pages 163 and 164 as guides.)

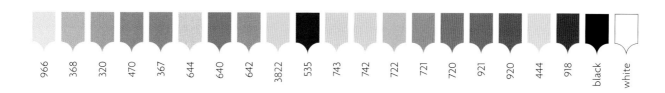

966 368 320 470 367 644 640 642 3822 535 743 742 722 721 720 921 920 444 918 black white

PROJECT 18: THREE FISH

(page 166)
Dimensions: 23 x 12 inches
Embroidered by Lee Sung-Hee, Korea

This hanging scroll is modeled after a master design for the ten-panel screen, *Unity*, which was completed by the author in the 1960s for the presidential mansion in Korea (pages 72–73). The fish motif has enjoyed a long history of representation in East Asian art and evokes a number of symbolic meanings. In a fourth-century BC Daoist text, the sage Zhuangzi eulogizes the joy and freedom of fish as they swim in a river, and fish have remained closely associated with personal freedom in Daoist thought. The word for fish in Chinese, *yu,* is a homonym for "abundance," and the large number of eggs laid by fish also rendered them symbolic of fertility. The image of a fish jumping out of water became a metaphor for a scholar's success in the prestigious civil service examinations and subsequent rise in the governmental bureaucracy, and leaping fish were frequently depicted in the art owned and used by scholars and officials, such as Qing rank badges and jade carvings.

MATERIALS
Fabric: Cotton/polyester blend
Thread: Empress or Splendor or
Au ver a Soie.

FOR ADVANCED EMBROIDERERS:
The embroiderer of three fish used hand-twisted thread on the scales of the fish, with 10 filaments twisted into one thread with a thickness of about 0.5 millimeters. The fins called for the thinnest thread, with 5 filaments twisted into one hairlike thread of about 0.2 millimeters. On her *Unity* screen, the author twisted yellow silk thread with gray and stitched it onto the bellies of the fish; the yellow helped create a golden sheen. If you use hand-twisted silk try Japanese Kamaito.

STITCHERY

Step 1 The water weeds should be stitched before fish A and B, starting at the top with Group 1 and ending at the bottom with Group 5. (**NOTE:** Fish C, which is partially hidden by water weeds, must be stitched prior to the weeds. Skip to Steps 7–22 for instructions on how to stitch fish C, then return to Step 1 for completion of the water weeds.) Use outline stitch (page 60) for the main water plant stems, but leave tails as a part of the stitch (page 74). Each group of weeds must be stitched over the previous group, overlapping stitches as when creating pine needles.

Step 2 As with pine needles, the color of the weeds determines the perspective of the picture: the water weeds in the foreground must be darker to create a three-dimensional effect. For the weeds, start with Group 1 (page 169) at the top, using light green #966. For the rest of the weeds in Group 1 use dark green #368. While the instructions have been simplified, feel free to follow the master work and choose more shades of greens than are provided here. Always use the lightest shades at the top (or background) and gradually change to darker shades toward the bottom. Each group should get progressively darker as you embroider down to the bottom (or foreground) of the piece.

Step 3 Repeat the above for Group 2, using green #368.

Step 4 For Group 3, use green #320.

Step 5 For Group 4, use #470.

Step 6 For Group 5, use #367.

Step 7 All the fish are embroidered in satin stitch, except for the outlines on the scales (for padding on the contours), and the belly is stitched in irregular satin stitches in the horizontal direction. Use the outline stitch for all contours of the scales, and use the same thread for the finishing stitchery (page 169).

Step 8 The heads of fish A and C are rendered in irregular straight satin stitch, using light gray #644 and dark gray #640. (Refer to page 166 and work in progress on page 169 for shading. See also this book's front cover.)

Step 9 Use medium gray #642 near the mouth and on the belly areas.

Step 10 For the lips, use yellow #3822.

Step 11 The scales on the backs of fish A and C are stitched in three shades of gray: #640, #642, #644 (page 169).

Step 12 As a highlight or accent on the scales, use darker gray #535 in three to five (or more, if desired) straight stitches of irregular lengths in the fan-shaped area where the scales overlap.

Step 13 The two yellow-beige tones (#743 and #742) in alternating stitches on the belly area create visual warmth as well as a sculptural effect.

Step 14 The fins of the two gray fish are first stitched in satin stitch with yellow-beige #743, leaving the ends ragged and uneven. Apply accents of dark gray #640 using straight stitches every third or fourth stitch. Do the same for the tail. Mix in additional accent colors, if desired.

Step 15 For fish B, or the red fish, use five shades of brownish-red: light red #722 and 721, medium red #720, dark red #921, and darker red #920 for accents on the neck and curved tail, just before the tail fin.

Step 16 For the outline stitches on the scales of the red fish use red #721. For the accent color on the fan-shaped area of the scales, embroider several straight stitches of irregular lengths in darker red #920.

Step 17 For the head of the red fish use brownish-red #721 on the forehead and #720 on the back of the head.

Step 18 For the belly of the red fish, use yellow-red #742 on the edge and #444 in the area where the red scales meet the body in the middle, in an irregular satin stitch in the horizontal direction (see front cover).

Step 19 For the fins of the red fish, use the same color as the belly, #742, in long irregular satin stitches, leaving the ends ragged and uneven. Accent the fins with straight stitches in #918 every four stitches or so. Do the same for the tail, but insert an additional accent shade of #921 using straight stitch.

Step 20 For the "nostrils" on the fish, apply a few satin stitches in black.

Step 21 For the eyes: stitch the whites first, followed by the black pupil over top of the white, then a white accent in the middle of the pupil, all completed in horizontal satin stitch.

Step 22 For the gills: stitch over the scales with medium red #720 and yellow #444, alternating the colors. The whiskery feelers beneath the eyes are done in yellow #444 (page 166).

Group 1

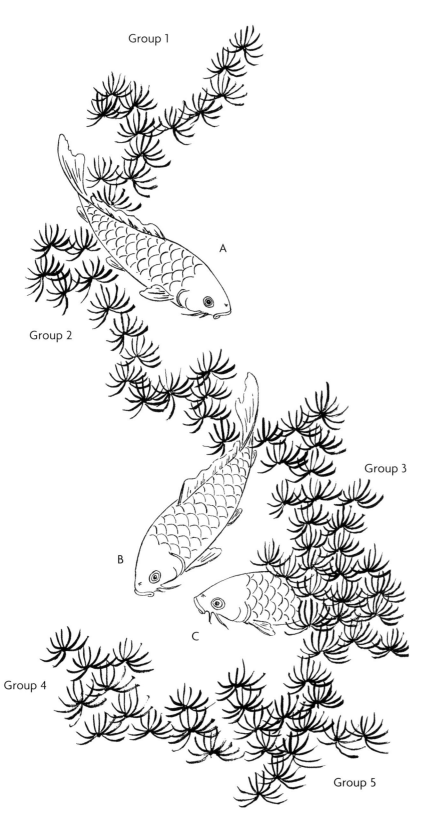

Group 2

A

B

C

Group 3

Group 4

Group 5

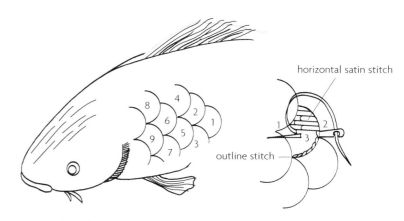

horizontal satin stitch

outline stitch

8		4	
	6	2	1
9	5		3
	7		

Fish-Scale Technique

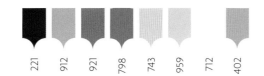

221 912 921 798 743 959 712 402

PROJECT 19: "HAPPY TALK" CELLULAR PHONE CASE

(pages 170 and 171)
Dimensions: 8 x 2 ¼ inches
Embroidered by Lee Byung-Sook, Korea

The author designed this cellular phone case using the three Korean characters most popularly used in textile design: *hee*, meaning "happiness," on the front face of the case; *su*, meaning "longevity"; and *bok*, meaning "fortune," on the back of the case. The little window in the case, where the caller's number appears, is surrounded with a thunderline pattern.

MATERIALS

Fabric: 65% silk/35% nylon-blend, navy blue
Thread: Soie de Paris or six-ply embroidery floss DMC (tightly twisted thread must be used for durability); Japan gold thread #8 or Kreinik gold metallic

STITCHERY

Step 1 Complete all stitchery in diagonal satin stitch.

Step 2 For the thunderline motif around the case window, start with magenta #221 and, proceeding clockwise, stitch the rest of the colors: green #912, red-brown #921,

blue #798, yellow #743, blue-green #959, blue #798, white #712 (page 172).

Step 3 For the *hee* character beneath the thunderline, use white #712, yellow #743, and beige #402 (page 172).

Step 4 For the *su* and *bok* characters on the back, use white #712 and beige #402 (page 172).

Step 5 All edges are finished with gold couching. Use two threads of Japan gold #8 side by side; couching thread is red. For a simpler method, use outline stitch in Kreinik gold.

Step 6 To make the mesh lining (page 170, right) into which the phone is inserted, you will need #22-mesh needlepoint canvas and ribbon with bias cut, about a ¾-inch wide. The lining, as pictured, is actual size—measure and cut the mesh to fit. Two pockets at each end hold the cell phone in place. Sew these on, followed by ribbon border. Sew ribbon around the edge using simple stitches. Place the lining on top of the finished embroidered case and cut to fit, leaving an extra ¾ inch all around for folding over and attaching to the lining.

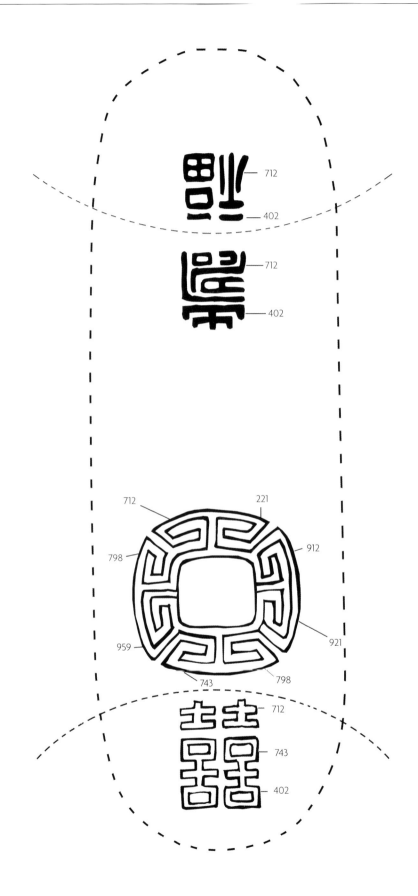

LIST OF SUPPLIERS

The Edwardian Needle
225 Belleville Avenue
Bloomfield, NJ 07003
tel: 973-743-9833
fax: 973-680-1162
www.theedwardianneedle.com.
e-mail: edwneedle.com

Fireside Stitchery
490 Lancaster Avenue
Frazer, PA 19355
toll free: 1-800-531-2607
tel: 610-889-9835
fax: 610-889-3013
www.firesidestitchery.com
e-mail: ria@firesidestitchery.com

Kreinik Mfg. Co., Inc.
3106 Lord Baltimore Drive, Suite 101
Baltimore, MD 21244
toll free: 1-800-537-2166
tel: 410-281-0040
fax: 410-281-2519
www.kreinik.com

Nordic Needle
1314 Gateway Drive
Fargo, ND 58103
toll free: 1-800-433-4321
tel: 701-235-5231
fax: 701-235-0952
www.nordicneedle.com

Needle Arts Inc.
2211 Monroe
Dearborn, MI 48124
toll free: 1-800-813-3103
tel: 313-278-6266
fax: 313-278-9227
www.shaypendray.com
e-mail: shaypendray@worldnet.att.net

IN KOREA:

Chung Young Yang Embroidery Museum
 Art Shop
53-12 Chungpa dong
2 ka, Yongsan-ku
Seoul, Korea 140-742
tel: 82-2-710-9133-9134
fax: 82-2-710-9267
e-mail: stella@sookmyung.co.kr.

STITCHERY TECHNIQUE NAMES IN CHINESE, KOREAN, AND JAPANESE

Please note that although the following list includes the most commonly used terms in three languages, the names of the various stitches may vary from region to region and even from embroiderer to embroiderer.

CHINESE

Dan tao, Ping tao zhen, Chang duan gou—
 variations of the long and short stitch
Dazi—seed stitch
Die lin—variation of the long and short stitch
Ding xian xiu—simple couching stitch
Ding zhen—gold couching stitch
Dui xiu—padding stitch
Heng ping zhen xiu—horizontal satin stitch
Na xiu—counted stitch on gauze
Pan qu zhen—piled loop stitch
Ping xiu—covering satin stitch
Purong xiu—weave stitch
Suo lian xiu—chain stitch
Tiao hua—various cross stitches
Wan xiu—holding loop stitch
Wang xiu—various net stitches
Xian wen zhen xiu—outline stitch
Xie ping zhen xiu—diagonal satin stitch

KOREAN

Jangsik su—decorative stitch
Jari su—mat stitch
Jaryun su—long and short stitch
Jick su—straight satin stitch
Jinggum su—couching stitch
Karyum su—leaf stitch
Maedup su—seed stitch
Pyung su—covering satin stitch
Sasul su—chain stitch
Socksim su—padding stitch
Yieum su—outline stitch

JAPANESE

Hippari nui—decorative patterned stitch
Hira nui—flat covering (satin) stitch
Komatori nui—couching with metallic thread
Kaeshi-nui—"staggered stitch" (outline stitch)
Nikuire nui—padding stitch
Nuiikiri—diagonal or vertical satin stitch
Sagara nui—seed or knot stitch
Sashi nui—long and short stitch
Wari nui—divided stitch

SELECTED BIBLIOGRAPHY

Baker, Muriel, and Margaret Lunt. *Blue and White: The Cotton Embroidery of Rural China*. London: Hazel Watson & Viney, Ltd., 1977.

Blum, Dilys. *The Fine Art of Textiles: The Collections of the Philadelphia Museum of Art*. Philadelphia: The Philadelphia Museum of Art, 1997.

Chatterton, Jocelyn. *Chinese Silks and Sewing Tools*. London: Allison & Wilcox, Ltd., 2002.

Chung, Young Yang. *The Art of Oriental Embroidery*. New York: Charles Scribner's Sons, 1979.

Chung, Young Yang, and Kim Tae-Ja. *Embroidery of Yesterday and Today*. Seoul: Sookmyung Women's University, 2000.

Chung, Young Yang. "The Origins and Historical Development of the Embroidery of China, Japan and Korea." Ph.D. diss. Ann Arbor, MI: UMI, A Bell & Howell Company, 1976.

Colton, Virginia, editor. *Reader's Digest Complete Guide to Needlework*. Pleasantville, NY: Reader's Digest Association, 1979.

Dawson, Barbara. *Metal Thread Embroidery*. New York: Taplinger Publishing Company, 1968.

D'Harcourt Raoul. *Textiles of Ancient Peru and Their Techniques*. Mineola, NY: Dover Publications, 1962.

Dowdey, Patrick, editor. *Threads of Light: Chinese Embroidery from Suzhou and the Photography of Robert Glenn Ketchum*. Los Angeles: UCLA Fowler Museum of Cultural History, 1999.

Gao, Hanyu. *Chinese Textile Designs*. Translated by Rosemary Scott and Susan Whitfield. London: Penguin Books, 1992.

Gillow, John, and Bryan Sentence. *World Textiles: A Visual Guide to Traditional Techniques*. Boston, New York and London: Little, Brown and Company, 1999.

Hong Kong Museum of Art. *Heavens' Embroidered Cloths: One Thousand Years of Chinese Textiles*. Hong Kong: Urban Council of Hong Kong, 1995.

Krody, Sumaru Belger. *Flowers of Silk and Gold: Four Centuries of Ottoman Embroidery*. London: Merrell Publishers, 2000.

Meller, Susan, and Joost Elffers. *Textile Designs: Two Hundred Years of European and American Patterns for Printed Fabrics Organized by Motif, Style, Color, Layout, and Period*. New York: Harry N. Abrams, Inc., 1991.

Meng, Ho Wing. *Straits Chinese Beadwork and Embroidery: A Collector's Guide*. Singapore: Times Books International, 1987.

Nichols, Marion. *Encyclopedia of Embroidery Stitches Including Crewel*. Mineola, NY: Dover Publications, 1974.

Parker, Mary. *Sashiko: Easy and Elegant Japanese Designs for Decorative Machine Embroidery*. Asheville, NC: Lark Books, 1999.

Richter, Paula Bradstreet. *Painted with Thread: The Art of American Embroidery*. Boston: Peabody Essex Museum, 2000.

Rust, Graham. *Graham Rust's Needlepoint Designs*. New York: Harry N. Abrams, Inc., 1998.

Scott, Philippa. *The Book of Silk*. London: Thames and Hudson, 1993.

Stevens, Helen M. *Embroidered Butterflies*. North Pomfret, VT: Trafalgar Square Books, 2001.

Synge, Lanto. *Art of Embroidery: History of Style and Technique*. Woodbridge, England: Antique Collector's Club, 2001.

Taylor, Roderick. *Embroidery of the Greek Islands*. New York: Interlink Books, 1998.

Taylor, Roderick. *Ottoman Embroidery*. New York: Interlink Books, 1993.

Trilling, James. *Aegean Crossroads: Greek Island Embroideries in the Textile Museum*. Washington: The Textile Museum, 1983.

Wang, Yarong. *Chinese Folk Embroidery*. Hong Kong: Commercial Press, 1985 (in Chinese).

Watts, Pamela. *Embroidered Flowers*. London: B. T. Batsford, Ltd., 1997..

ACKNOWLEDGMENTS

I could never have completed this book without the generous help and support of a great many people. At Harry N. Abrams, Inc., I would like to thank the editor-in-chief Eric Himmel for his understanding of the art of embroidery; my editor Andrea Danese for her devotion and commitment to the arduous task of simplifying the instructions for beginning embroiderers; Karyn Gerhard for her inception of this volume and her assistance in the research for embroidery materials; and Darilyn L. Carnes to whom I am grateful for the beautiful design of this book. My grateful thanks also go to Marie Campbell for writing such kind words about me in her foreword.

I invited Kim Tae-Ja, chief curator at Chung Young Yang Embroidery Museum in Korea, to coordinate the creation of the masterworks seen in the photographs for the projects in this book. I owe her thanks for her efforts and undivided attention to the embroiderers. I am pleased with the results and want to thank all who worked on the projects, including longtime friends; former students from the International Embroidery Institute in Korea; friends with whom I have lectured; and master embroiderers from China, Hong Kong, and Korea. I am most grateful for their eagerness to participate and willingness to complete the projects on a tight schedule. My thanks to Kim Tae-Ja, world-renowned master embroiderer, for taking on *White Peacock with Peonies* with enthusiasm and for agreeing to try nylon metallic threads for the first time; to Dana Bloch, a member of EGA (The Embroiderers' Guild of America), for completing the sample embroidery that appears on page 66, her first experience in the gold couching technique in a small geometric shape; to Deborah Bowers, another EGA member, for traveling long distances to complete *Birds with Grasshopper on Orchid;* to Choi Jeong-In in Korea, who experimented with shading methods using textured threads in *Rose of Sharon;* to Lee Byung-Sook, who employed the traditional Korean embroidery techniques on *Celebration* and who accepted last-minute instructions over the phone for *Happy Talk;* to Lee Sung-Hee for her masterful rendering of *Three Fish,* especially for her water weeds, a new technique for her; to Lee Yun-Jeong, the director of the Myungga Traditional Costume Center in Dae-Jeon, Korea, for agreeing to oversee the creation of *Morning Glories* and her generous offer to frame the finished piece; to Kim Kum-Ja for embroidering *Morning Glories;* to P. C. Wang in Hong Kong for his kind contribution of *Magnolia II;* and to Jin Yuan Shan, director of the Textile Studio in Harbin City, China, for supervising the embroiderer who stitched *Hydrangea* using Western-made silk thread for the first time. I also thank Jin for accompanying me on my extensive research trip to Heilongjiang (old Manchuria) and to the studio of a Miao embroiderer.

At the museums, my thanks go to Dr. Ben Bronson at The Field Museum in Chicago for his kind attention and for allowing me access to the study room, and to John Weinstein for the care he took in taking photographs according to my specifications. To Tiliys Blum at the Philadelphia Museum of Art for allowing me to study the artifacts and providing valuable information about Western embroidery. Thanks to Chang Su-Herchins at the Smithsonian Institution for her valuable information on the collections; to Don Hurlbert of the Smithsonian for his photography; and to Susan Crawford, also at the Smithsonian, thanks for allowing me to study at the collection center. I am grateful to Jennifer Heimbecker at The Textile Museum for furnishing me with transparencies on such short notice. My thanks to Nobuko Kajitani at The Metropolitan Museum of Art for sharing her technical advice and expertise. Most of all, my deepest appreciation goes to Valrae Reynolds at The Newark Museum for her kind attention to my study there and for helping me obtain transparencies. I am grateful to Chris Hall for making transparencies of his precious collection for this book. I also owe thanks to TiTi Halle at Cora Ginsburg, LLC, for sharing her expertise in Western embroidery techniques and kindly lending the illustrations. I am grateful to Shin Tak-Keun, director of the Onyang Folk Museum in Korea, for his advice and for providing me with the latest information on Korean textiles. My sincere thanks to Dr. Yu Hee-Kyung for her advice on the costumes, and to Mr. Lee Kang-Chil of Korea for his suggestions and advice. Thanks to Hea-Kyum Kim at Christie's and to Tina Zhonars, head of the Chinese department, for allowing me to illustrate important works of art. Thanks also goes to Duk Sang-Lee in Korea and Anjian Wang for their assistance. I also owe thanks to James Tigerman for his assistance on our research trips to museums. Most of all, I am grateful to Feng Zhao at the China National Silk Museum in Nanjing for accompanying me on my study trips to the various embroidery studios and museums in China.

My warm thanks to Nam-Hee Gong, Ph.D., director of the Korean Cultural Center in New York, for her help in my research; to Diana Collins for introducing me to the silk museum in Suzhou and for her efforts in making sure my trip to China was productive; to Don J. Cohn for getting involved despite his busy schedule by providing me with copies of the newest publications from China; to Dr. Robert Hamburger and his wife, Marilyn, for assisting in my research in Boston; to John T. Ma and Cicelia Poon for their patience and translation of Chinese texts; and to my good friend Judith Rutherford for her never-ending search for new embroidery techniques and to Ken Rutherford for his efforts to ensure our safety during our trips.

My heartfelt thanks must be conveyed to John Bigelow Taylor and Dianne Dubler for their supreme efforts in creating exquisite photographs for this book; to Maggie Nimkin for her gorgeous photography; to Yim Won-Soon and Han Seok-Hong for their photography during my brief visit in Korea. My thanks also goes to Lee Talbot, who has been studying silk embroidery and the embroidered textiles as his elective study for a number of years with me, for his dedication and patience in typing the manuscript for this volume. I am grateful to Norell Guttman for his generous time and patience looking after my computer, and to Jun H. Choi for translating my hand-drawn illustrations and diagrams into computer-drawn files. Thanks also to John McKenna for his drawing of *Magnolia II* and for assistance with many of the illustrations. Thanks to Edith Cheng in Hong Kong and Noriko Gonsho in Japan, and to Wang Yarong for the lesson in holding, or Pekingese, stitch.

For their encouragement in my endeavors I would like to thank: Barbara Tober, chairman of Museum of Arts and Design, and David McFadden, curator; Joyce Denney of The Metropolitan Museum of Art; Camill Cook, president of Friends of Fiber Arts International; Dr. Colin MacKenzie, associate director and curator at the Asia Society; Dr. John M. Lundquist, chief librarian of the Asian and Middle East division of the New York Public Library; and finally to Dr. Lee Kyung-Sook, president of the Sookmyung Women's University in Korea.

And most of all, my thanks go to my ever-patient husband, Ken, and to my sister, Jee-Yang, for their boundless support.

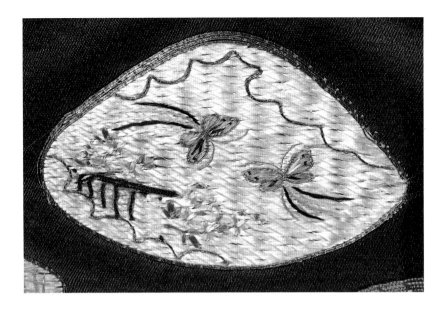

Editor: Andrea Danese
Designer: Darilyn Lowe Carnes
Production Manager: Jane Searle

Library of Congress Cataloging-in-Publication Data

Chung, Young Yang.
  Painting with a needle : learning the art of silk
embroidery / with Young Yang Chung.
    p. cm.
Includes index.
  ISBN 0–8109–4570–3
  1. Embroidery—East Asia. 2. Embroidery—
Patterns. 3. Silk thread.
  I. Title.

TT769.E18 C48 2003
746.44—dc21
                    2003000296

Published in 2003 by Harry N. Abrams,
Incorporated, New York. All rights reserved.
No part of the contents of this book may be
reproduced without written permission of
the publisher.

Printed and bound in Italy
10 9 8 7 6 5 4 3 2 1

 Harry N. Abrams, Inc.
100 Fifth Avenue
New York, N.Y. 10011
www.abramsbooks.com

Abrams is a subsidiary of
LA MARTINIÈRE
G R O U P E

PHOTO CREDITS

PHOTOGRAPHERS
Maggie Nimkin: 1, 14, 34, 43, 45 (top), 49, 51, 53,
    59, 60, 61, 63 (top), 65, 68, 70, 76, 79, 80, 99,
    127, 150
John Bigelow Taylor: 2–3, 6, 15 (bottom), 23–26, 31,
    33, 36 (bottom), 37, 40, 44, 45 (bottom), 46–48,
    52, 54, 55, 57, 64, 66, 71–73, 77, 78, 81–83, 90,
    96, 97 (top), 98, 100, 104, 110, 113, 114, 118, 129,
    137, 138, 140–141, 145, 151, 154–156, 163
John Weinstein: 8
Yim Won-Soon: 19
Don Hurlbert: 28
Han Seok-Hong: 39
Young Yang Chung: 88, 91

COLLECTIONS
Collection of the author: 14, 19, 23, 24, 26, 27, 33,
    34, 36 (bottom), 40, 46–48, 49, 52 (right, top
    and bottom), 53, 57 (right), 59, 60, 63 (top), 64,
    65, 69, 70, 71, 76, 79, 80, 90
Collection of the Chung Young Yang Embroidery
    Museum at Sookmyung Women's University,
    Korea. 15 (bottom), 31, 37, 39, 44, 55, 57 (left),
    61, 68, 72, 73, 77, 78, 81
Collection of Chris Hall, Hong Kong: 20, 32
Collection of The Field Museum, Chicago: 8
Collection of the Sookmyung Women's University
    Museum, Korea: 15 (top)
Collection of Eskenazi, Ltd., London: 16
Collection of the Dunhuang Research Institute,
    Gansu, China: 21
Collection of the Smithsonian Institution,
    National Museum of Natural History,
    Washington, D.C.: 28, 54, 127

Collection of The Newark Museum of Art: 29
Collection of Christie's, New York: 36 (top), 63
    (bottom), 67
Collection of The Textile Museum, Washington,
    D.C. Gift of the Mrs. Philip Hoffman Founda-
    tion: 41
Collection of The Textile Museum, Washington,
    D.C. Gift of Mrs. Fred S. Gichner: 42
Collection of The Metropolitan Museum of Art,
    New York: 43
Collection of the Philadelphia Museum of Art.
    Gift of Mrs. Hampton L. Carson, 1929: 58
Collection of the Philadelphia Museum of Art.
    Gift of the Friends of the Philadelphia
    Museum of Art, 1988: 75
Collection of Cora Ginsberg, LLC, New York:
    62, 69
Collection of Dana Bloch, New York: 66

Page 17: After *Origin of Chinese National Cos-
    tume*, p. 25

NOTES TO THE TEXT

1. Young Yang Chung, "The Origins and Historical
    Development of the Embroidery of China,
    Japan, and Korea" (Ph.D. diss., Ann Arbor, MI:
    UMI, A Bell & Howell Company, 1976), 9.
2. Young Yang Chung, *The Art of Oriental Embroi-
    dery* (New York: Charles Scribner's Sons,
    1979), 22.
3. Chung, "The Origins and Historical Develop-
    ment," 143.

Fukusa, detail, see caption, page 36

Endpapers:
Ten-Panel Screen, depicting *baek soo* and
baek bok (Koren, 19th century). This screen,
depicting the highly stylized Chinese characters of *soo* (long life) and *bok* (abundant
luck), is used for birthday celebrations. It is
embroidered entirely in diagonal stitch.

Binding case, front:
Author's signature, see caption, page 99

Binding case, back:
Pillow End Piece (Korean, 19th century).
This leopard, a Korean military symbol,
is surrounded by bats, and a thunderline
pattern in the outer circle encompasses
the piece. This collection of motifs and
their placement in the design is typical
of Korea.